Laurence S
Arnhem Path

Jan Scott

BARNTHORN
PUBLISHING

Published by Barnthorn Publishing Limited.

ISBN: 978-1-917120-11-1

For Peggy and Laurie.
It was a privilege and an honour to have you as my mum and dad.

So, I guess the question is, was the armada into Arnhem in September 1944 worth it?

And why do we commemorate with such passion what history has cruelly consigned into the bracket of defeat?

Well, if I tell you that to this day my soldiers still cry "remember Arnhem" when they charge into the contemporary peril of bullet or bomb, you might start to understand what it means.

Lieutenant General Andrew Harrison DSO MBE
Colonel Commandant The Parachute Regiment, Ginkel Heath,
September 2023

ACKNOWLEDGMENTS

Writing a book is always a team effort and this book relied on many people's help and contributions. I'm very grateful to the following: my cousin, Jean Abbott, whose extensive research on our family discovered the history of Laurence's grandparents, and important events in his parent's lives. Lieutenant General Harrison DSO MBE, of the Parachute Regiment, kindly allowed me to quote from his moving speech given at the 2023 Arnhem Commemorations. Jon Baker, Curator of the Airborne Assault Museum, for his contribution about meeting Laurence when he visited the superb Airborne Assault Museum at IWM Duxford.

Dr Clare Smith, Historic Collection Curator, Metropolitan Police Museum, enabled me to find out a lot about Laurence's police career. Paul Bickley, of the Metropolitan Police Crime Museum, helped with contacts and kindly enabled me to see Laurence's medals again. Roy Medcalf and Bob Fenton, both sent me vivid stories about Laurence during his police service. Authors, Peter Gijbels and David Truesdale, for their book *Leading the Way to Arnhem*, which is recommended as a thoroughly detailed history of the 21st Independent Parachute Company and its brave soldiers. A heartfelt thanks goes to all the past members of the 21st Independent Parachute Company Club.

Deepest thanks to the following for their help and support with this book's journey, Dave Allen, Linda Bailey, Vivienne Daniell, Annie Gooch MBE, Ben Hill, Heather Johnson, Adam Jowett, John Lazenby MBE, Peter Marks, and Erny van Wijk.

Lastly, but certainly not least, grateful thanks to the publishers, Ashley Barnett and Neil Thornton of Barnthorn Publishing Limited, for their support in publishing the book, and enabling my father's story to go out into the world.

CONTENTS

1

FROM REFUGEES TO RESILIENCE

In the Spring of 1920, as Emma Solomon cradled her new born son, Laurence, in her arms, she couldn't know that, for him, the future would be one of life-threatening situations, requiring bravery beyond duty. He was born on 13 March 1920, in Islington, a densely populated, bustling part of North London. The family were still recovering from their experiences of the First World War and surviving the influenza pandemic that had swept through the world, and there was no doubt that Laurence was born into one of the most tumultuous times in history. It shaped his personality, his morality and gave him a resilience which he'd need, as unknown to the family, ahead lay some of the most terrifying times the world had ever faced.

Laurence's parents already had to face their own challenges before they even got married. Laurence's father, Morris Solomon was born on 29 January 1885, to refugee parents who had fled for their lives from the Russian Pogroms. In the early 1880s, Laurence's grandparents, Lazarus and Rachel and their children, had packed what few possessions they had and boarded a ship in Lithuania, seeking refuge and a new life in the smoke-filled, crowded East End of London.

When Morris was born, the family was living in three rooms at the Rothschild Buildings in Whitechapel, a tenement block built to house poorer Jewish refugees from Eastern Europe. As he grew up, Morris turned his back on practising the religion, leading to him being ostracised from his family, particularly his mother. His father, Lazarus, had died when Morris was just seven-years-old.

He moved into lodgings with the Brettell family, living near City Road, and it was while he was here, he grew fond of one of the daughters, Emma. His lodgings were not far from his family and it would be nice to think he'd still kept in contact with some of his siblings, maybe meeting them secretly in cafes, or writing to them. One clue may be that Laurence did know his Uncle Simon, one of Morris's brothers.

As Morris and Emma grew closer, they would have little time to enjoy their deepening friendship. The clouds of war were growing large on the horizon and their relationship was soon to be tested in a way they could never have imagined. After weeks of mounting tension, Britain declared war on Germany on 4 August 1914. Initially there was a patriotic rush to join the military and at the late age of twenty-nine, Morris joined up to the Dorsetshire Regiment, under the name of Harry Scott. Why he used a completely different name to enlist under is only to be guessed at.

The 'Dorsets' were an infantry regiment and Morris (Harry) was shipped out to France immediately. Emma was likely to have been doing some form of war work in London, and hoping there was truth in the rumour that the war would 'be over by Christmas' and Morris would be back soon. It was not to be. Only three months into the war, on 18 November Morris was listed as 'missing' on the casualty list issued by the War Office.

Not having any news of whether he was even still alive, must have been awful for Emma. It wasn't until April 1915, that Morris was listed on the International Red Cross List of Prisoners of War. He'd been captured at La Bassee, where the Dorsets had been fighting and was now listed as 'Soldat 6878' and interned at Munster Prisoner of War Camp in Germany. On the Red Cross records, Emma was listed as his next of kin, and she was finally told where Morris was on 12 May 1915: a very long, anxious time of waiting to find out what had happened to the man with whom she was falling in love.

Four years Morris spent as a prisoner. It can only be imagined what mental and physical strength it took to survive: forced to work as slave labour in salt mines, which caused him to lose his teeth, and suffer from malnutrition. When the Armistice for 'The Great War' was declared in November 1918, Morris was finally freed and returned to Emma in London. He was awarded the 1914 Star, the British War Medal and the Victory Medal.

Could it have been his love for Emma that had kept Morris motivated to survive the camp? It seemed to be, because as soon as they were reunited, they lost no time in getting married on a warm summer's day on 16 June 1919 at Holborn Registry Office. But life still wasn't easy. Along with thousands of other war veterans, Morris hadn't returned to Prime Minister Lloyd George's promise of a 'land fit for heroes'. The British political landscape was changing and the economy was struggling with the cost of the war and high unemployment and in 1924, the political left had their first Labour Prime Minister, Ramsey McDonald.

Living in London, Morris and Emma had more work opportunities. Morris was packing china for J. Lyons Company, a company specialising in hospitality and food. It was a steady job but probably quite low paid. The couple needed this steady income, as they had moved to Florence Street, Islington, to be able to rent more rooms, as Emma had fallen pregnant and they were starting a family. The birth of their first baby boy, Laurence, must have brought great joy to the couple after fate seemingly testing them to the limits, and in time Laurence was joined by two brothers, Mark and Danny, and a much-loved sister Rae.

But, as Morris and Emma celebrated Laurence's birth, neither of them could know that only nineteen years later, the storm clouds of war would gather over Britain again. Laurence would need to draw on his family's experiences of survival and resilience as he would find himself fighting for his life in an enemy occupied country.

2

BECOMING AIRBORNE

'I was always running everywhere. I ran to school and back. Ran to work and back,' Laurence explained in later life, acknowledging that he was a natural athlete, having long legs and a lean frame. Leaving school, he took up an apprenticeship in the printing trade, training to be a Heidelburg printing press operator and likely to have been in a company located in Fleet Street, which was the centre of the printing trade and newspapers at the time. The trade unions were very organised in the print trade, this experience, and seeing the effect of the economic depression, probably gave Laurence his political beliefs. He was always a traditional Labour Party and trade union supporter, and remained so all his life.

The family had moved again, this time to Central Street, still in Islington, London, and the run to work and back kept Laurence fit enough to be a competitive athlete, winning a medal for coming first in a 440 yd, quarter of a mile race (now the 400 m). Unknown to him at the time, it was to be his last race. The date engraved on his medal was 1939, and on 3 September that year, the Prime Minister, Neville Chamberlain, in a sombre broadcast on the radio, declared that the country was at war with Germany.

Laurence's winner's medal 1939
(Jan Scott)

As the Solomon family heard the news, they must have felt a rush of emotions and anxiety: Laurence's dad Morris, remembering the horrors of the last war, and Emma, recalling her long, anxious wait for years to know that Morris had survived. Now they were facing the prospect of their sons being called up to fight in another world war.

For a fit, motivated young man, however, Laurence found himself eager to fight, receiving his call up papers and joining the army on 20 June 1940 and joining a battalion formed of young volunteers. In a written article he called *My Early Days in the Army*, he recounted his experiences and thoughts of his time in this battalion. (The author warns the reader to note that in Laurence's written recollections and interviews, he uses the language prevalent at the time of the Second World War, and refers to the 'German Army', 'Boche' and 'Hun'). He recalls:

In the spring of 1940, the War Office decided to accept volunteers for the Army aged eighteen and over. A number of special recruiting offices were opened throughout the country and those passing the medical were formed into Battalions of many of the County regiments. These became the 8th (young soldier) Battalions of the Regiments concerned and were not considered for duty overseas but, after initial training, were earmarked for Home Defence. Many of these units became known as the 'Borstal Battalions', as they all seemed to consist of a number of unruly and immature teenagers and only a minority were genuinely interested in becoming efficient soldiers and whose main desire was to see some action.

Laurence was one of that minority who was actually interested in becoming an efficient soldier. The 8th Battalion he joined was that of the Dorsetshire Regiment, coincidentally the same regiment as his father had joined in the First World War. It can only be guessed at what Morris thought of his son joining: maybe a mixture of pride, but also terrible fear and anxiety. It seems Laurence may also have had in his mind the experiences of his father and the infantry in the last war. He soon became frustrated at being 'stuck' in this battalion with its lack of professional, modern weapons, uniforms and officers he regarded as too young or stuck in their past military experience of the last war. He didn't hold back on his views, as in *My Early Days in the Army* he describes his experience and the trials of being one of the 'PBI: Poor Bloody Infantry,' as he called them. He wrote:

I remember the 8th Battalion Dorsetshire Regiment well 'What a shower!' In the summer of 1941, we were relieved from the trenches we had dug and occupied on the beaches of the Weymouth area since June 1940: our task being to repulse invasion by the dreaded Boche. It's just as well they didn't come as we had but ten rounds each for our antiquated P.14 rifles, (the British service rifle from 1914) and were using one bayonet between two. Our Boyes [sic] Anti-Tank rifle was a broom handle and our 2-inch mortar was a lump of wood with a Vim carton attached to it.

To cap it all we wore denims as there was no battledress yet available for the likes of us. We had no cap badges and we route-marched regularly through the local villages to show the flag and keep up the morale of the local people. Our success in this latter regard was indicated by the motto adopted by the local people "Thank God we've got a Navy". I'm convinced they looked upon us as being escapees from the Borstal on Portland nearby. So keen were the embryo soldiers amongst us to create an impression that we saluted everyone–postmen, policemen, even dustmen.

Our route marches always seemed to take us to Stonehenge, giving me the strong suspicion that we were in fact a special sacrificial Battalion. Those of us who really wanted to get into the war volunteered for everything in our desire to leave the Battalion–girl guides, even the U-boat service–all to no avail.

When we were at last relieved from our duties on the beaches, we marched from Weymouth to Piddlehinton, near Dorchester. Dressed in full battle order, with our broomstick and Vim carton rifle at the slope. It poured with rain throughout and we arrived at Piddlehinton around midnight, to the first 'Spider' camp any of us had ever seen. It seemed like the Ritz hotel–showers with hot water and a clean cookhouse which served us, even at this late hour, with the best cooked meal we'd tasted for months. We finally got into our bunks, clean and refreshed but dog-tired, at 1.30 am Thankfully we closed our eyes.

Of course, it was too good to last and at 3 am we were awakened by bells, bugles, sirens and shouted commands–the General Alarm for Invasion had been received, indicating the Germans had landed in England, and our superiors were reacting in time honoured fashion, "When in danger, fear, or doubt, run in circles, scream and shout!"

I dragged myself from my warm bed, reassembled my equipment and paraded outside. Within minutes I was soaked to the skin –even my socks. Platoon Commanders were summoned to an 'O' group, leaving the P.B. standing in the pouring rain, fed up to the back teeth and praying for a quick surrender–by us or the Germans–we didn't care which! Some thirty minutes later Our Young Subaltern (OYS) returned. He was about 18.

Laurence's views of some of his officers were certainly somewhat critical, expressing concern that many were entering the Second World

War expecting it to be like the first. He wrote:

> The Company and Battalion Commanders, on the other hand, all gave the impression they'd been dragged out of a sleepy retirement, wore World War 1 (some went so far as to say Crimean or Boer War) style uniforms, liberally patched with chunks of leather over moth-holes... Most of them were at a loss to understand what had happened to all the horses.

Laurence would not know that in a few years he would play a major part in Field Marshal Montgomery's plan Operation Market Garden, but his remarks about the competency of his battalion officers and resources gave an idea of his views. He makes the comment 'These... (officers)... incidentally were part, as was the Battalion, of the Brigade commanded at that time by a certain Brigadier Montgomery–makes you think, doesn't it?'

What he wrote next showed his love of being cheeky and challenging towards his officers and bosses, an attitude which lasted all his life:

> Our Young Subaltern (OYS) gathered us, his platoon around him, sitting us down in the many puddles and with a voice charged with emotion announced, 'I will put you in the picture. The dreaded Hun Paratroopers have landed at Warminster and our Battalion is to force march there and contain them until Monty's other Battalions can carry out a right and left flanking movement and destroy them. Any questions?'
>
> There was an ominous silence. Normally no-one dreamed of asking any questions–we were always too browned off and apathetic. On this occasion, I considered the prospect of a forced march of some thirty miles with some distaste and decided some sort of delaying tactic wouldn't come amiss. I stood up and took a pace forward, 'Sir, we have to force march to Warminster some thirty miles away?'
>
> OYS somewhat warily 'Yes, that's right!'
>
> 'Sir, we shall march at five miles per hour?'
>
> OYS even more warily: 'Yes, that's right.'
>
> 'Sir, if we march thirty miles at five miles per hour, would you agree it will take us about six hours to arrive?'

OYS still more warily, 'Yes, that's right.'

'Sir, don't you think that by the time we arrive the dreaded Hun Paratroops will have gone?'

The Platoon Sergeant shouted, 'Fall in two men. Prisoner and Escort to the guardroom, double MARCH!'

The sequel was that I, (as the prisoner) accompanied by my two escorts, travelled in comfort to Warminster in the Utility truck, whilst all the other poor b****rs had to leg it in the pouring rain. When the Battalion finally arrived at its destination, the enemy were nowhere to be found, if indeed there had ever been any.

The panic caused by the threat of enemy invasion led by the feared German paratroopers, the Fallschirmjäger, understandably gripped Britain. Nazi Germany had developed an elite fighting force of Paratroopers and used them, in 1940, to invade Norway, Denmark and the Netherlands.

Laurence's frustration with being in the 8th Battalion Dorsetshire Regiment led him to seize the chance to leave when volunteers were requested for transfer to the Royal Air Force to train as aircrew. However, as he soon found out, many of the transfers were cancelled. Doing anything to avoid going back to the Dorsets, Laurence accepted the offer of joining a new unit of the Army Air Corps (AAC): the Glider Pilot Regiment. Although he started training, he didn't pass his course of flying solo in a Tiger Moth, and so couldn't become a Glider Pilot. In later years he always explained that whilst in the aircraft, he had remarked to his flying instructor how proud he was that he'd executed a smooth landing in the Tiger Moth, to which the instructor remarked loudly, 'we are still airborne. You haven't landed yet!'

All was not lost, however. In 1940, Winston Churchill had been following the development and use of the Fallschirmjäger and decided that the British Army should also have a similar military capability. In February 1942, British paratroopers were used successfully in Operation Biting: a raid to capture enemy radar equipment near Bruneval, France, and bring it back to Britain. The raid was led by Major John Frost. By that August, the new Parachute Regiment was officially formed and became operational. In addition, Churchill and senior officers realised that future airborne operations would need to have a small unit of highly trained paratroopers to be parachuted in first. Their role was to be marking out the Dropping Zones (DZ) for the paratroopers and Landing Zones (LZ) for gliders: large engine-less aircraft, carrying men and equipment into battle, which would need to be towed for any forthcoming operations.

An elite pathfinder unit was needed. In June 1942, Major John Lander established the 21st Independent Parachute Company, the 21st IPC. A company eventually consisting of around 180 men, handpicked in consultation with his second-in-command, Captain 'Boy' Wilson. Laurence, the super fit athlete, with a personal resilience developed from his childhood, was an ideal candidate, and he was selected as one of the first members of this pathfinder unit. He was fighting fit, twenty-two years of age and raring to start the training to become one of the British Army's elite fighting soldiers.

In his book, *First In! Parachute Pathfinder Company*, Ron Kent, who was in 1 Platoon of the pathfinders, describes the training that Laurence had to do, along with other recruits. First, at Hardwick Hall in Derbyshire which had become the depot of the Parachute Regiment, and concerned with training and physical selection. This included a forced march of ten miles in two hours carrying and wearing full battle kit. Recruits had to crawl in mud whilst machine gun bullets whizzed over their heads. To get used to the force of impact on landing when jumping out of a plane, double physical training sessions were designed to train recruits to cope. On the non-physical learning side, potential recruits were taught about the construction and safety issues of parachutes, exiting an aircraft safely, and landing with 'feet and knees together.'

Hardwick Hall, Airborne Forces Depot, 1942. Laurence is far left.
(By permission of the Airborne Assault Museum, IWM Duxford)

After passing all the fitness and psychological tests, Laurence volunteered for the 'real' parachute course. He packed up his kit bag, and with some of the other trainee pathfinders, clambered into the personnel carrier: likely to have been a lorry with hard wooden benches. They all arrived at RAF Ringway, south of Manchester, now the site of Manchester Airport.

Here, as Ron Kent describes in his book, the training continued, initially as 'synthetic training' which in fact meant jumping out of empty fuselages of de-commissioned Whitley bombers onto thick mattresses. When the men got used to this, the next stage was actual parachute jumps: the dreaded balloon jumps, something that Laurence always remembered doing. This meant getting into a basket beneath a swaying barrage balloon, being hoisted to 800 ft then jumping out through a hole in the basket. At least it gave some feel of the pull of the chute, and landing properly, for next was on to real aircraft: jumping from low flying Whitley bombers, or 'flying coffins' as they became known due to the long box-like shape and the cramped space in which the men were packed before they jumped.

Laurence enjoyed the physical challenge and easily completed the jumps needed to earn his precious set of parachute wings which he carefully sewed onto his uniform proving he was a qualified paratrooper, an elite fighting soldier. Now it was the British paratroopers turn to become feared by the Nazi German Army. During their fierce fighting in North Africa, the red sand had clung to the tail straps of the British soldier's parachute smocks, and they became known as the 'rote teufeln': the 'Red Devils'.

For Laurence, engagement with the enemy was still some months away and as a pathfinder, he had more training specific to the unit's role of being sent in to battle first, and having to be self-sufficient fighting unit. This he'd learned at Larkhill, a garrison near Salisbury Plain and ironically near to Stonehenge, where he had been in the Dorsetshire Regiment, except now he considered himself, finally, to be 'in the real Army'. Along with other members of the 21st IPC, over the winter of 1942, he studied map reading, navigation, unarmed combat, went on day and night exercises, completed more parachute training jumps from Halifax bombers, and did a live exercise where gliders landed near to Stonehenge.

Laurence, Tunis 1943
(Jan Scott)

Finally in May 1943, the pathfinders were sent abroad. They travelled by ship to join the 1st Parachute Brigade in North Africa, landing in Oran in Algeria, but it wasn't plain sailing at all. Laurence, along with the other paratroopers, had to endure more training in the heat, lack of water, and the harsh winds of the terrain, and still there was no actual fighting to do. But learning to survive in such conditions would prove vital in the future when they, and Laurence, were surrounded by the enemy and fighting for their lives. From Algeria, they were later transferred via an uncomfortable cattle truck train ride into Tunisia where they stayed until September 1943, when, at last, they found out they were to be sent on a mission into the European theatre of war. Italy was looking like it was going to surrender, but the German Army, still in Italy, had absolutely no intention of surrendering and were still a fighting force.

3

THE ITALIAN JOB

The Italian Government surrendered on 8 September 1943, which enabled the Allies to land in southern Italy, but there was still the dangerous presence of the German Army which remained in the country, tasked with slowing down the Allies progress north through the country. Although trained to insert into battle from the air, Laurence and the pathfinders found themselves arriving in a Royal Navy convoy taking them from North Africa to Italy as part of Operation Slapstick. This was the code name for the arrival by sea by airborne soldiers from the 1st Airborne Division.

Once landed and in camp, Laurence's job, as part of 2 Platoon, was patrolling to find exactly where the German Army were, and only, if necessary, engage and eliminate any enemy they encountered. For Laurence it was the first time he'd come into contact with an active enemy whose main tactic was ambushing the Allied soldiers. Laurence later wrote about what happened:

> The 21st landed in Italy on 9 September 1943 having travelled from North Africa via HMS *Aurora*, a cruiser. Our base and company HQ was at Taranto. Our main duties were reconnaissance patrols travelling north along the east coast towards the retreating German Army.
>
> On one such patrol we consisted of two jeeps containing four of us and two DR's (despatch riders on motorcycles) with a Bren gun in each. I had a Bren gun. Our objective was to patrol the coast road north and if possible, contact the enemy. In charge was Captain Spivey of the 21st Independent Parachute Company. Mussolini certainly made some excellent main roads in this area. After North Africa, they were a joy to travel along. On this particular patrol we left Taranto at about 11 pm. It was

dark. Every few miles along the coast road were pill boxes manned by the Italian Army. We had no prior knowledge of this or the disposition of the German troops who were retreating slowly north wards.

Knowing that they were too lightly armed for intense fighting, Laurence's patrol group decided to use the tactic of driving as fast as possible, to evade any possible ambush from the enemy. With many Italians still not aware the British Army had landed, in the dark, the speeding patrol was automatically considered a German one. This confused the Italian soldiers stationed in the pillboxes along the road the patrol was travelling. Laurence continues:

> By the time we had reached the first pill box we were travelling at about 80 mph, and the lone sentry standing outside sprang smartly to attention, gave the Nazi salute and shouted "Heil Hitler". Discretion being the better part of valour, we returned the salute and the shout. The occupants of the next pill box had been forewarned and by the time we had reached it, the whole guard was on parade. Saluting and "Heil Hitlering", we returned the salutations. This farce continued along miles of coast road until we reached Barletta. We had passed through many villages and tried to get information from the inhabitants. We found that if the village square was empty when we arrived, then the Germans were not far away and we took appropriate precautions like driving like hell the opposite way. If the German's had gone, we were given a hero's welcome. "Viva Inglese!" with the hand V for victory sign and… (the local Italians) …asking "Why didn't you come sooner?"
>
> Eventually, still travelling north, we went past the point where we should have turned west, and stopped for refreshments on a ridge of hills. But not for long as below us in a crater about half a mile away was a German tank laager with scores of tanks and German crews looking busy, we immediately made a strategic withdrawal to the south.

As the skies lightened, the Italians could now see that the patrol was British. Laurence explained what happened:

Dawn had broken before 7 am and we stopped in the deserted square of a village. Within minutes we were surrounded and hemmed in by hundreds of Italian villagers. Wine was supplied and flowers thrown at us (sometime in pots from windows of tenement blocks). An American Italian told us that a German patrol came through the village at 7 am every morning. Captain Spivey said we would have to get rid of the villagers as we could not move. That was easy: a short sharp blast from a Bren gun and they disappeared within seconds. Relieved, I thought at least now we could get back to Taranto before the German patrol came. But no! Capt. Spivey posted the two Bren guns either side of the road, and the remaining troops taking up strategic positions behind. At 1 minute to 7 am we heard the noise of a large diesel vehicle approaching. My grip tightened on the Bren gun, I adjusted the sights and was ready for anything. We could see people hanging on the sides of the lorry holding weapons, and then the Italian flag appeared. About 20 Italians had commandeered a German medical vehicle and had come to join the Inglese. They had no idea how near they'd been to being wiped out.

Relieved the German patrol had not appeared, there was now the problem of the enthusiasm of the Italians who wanted to stay with the airborne soldiers. Laurence continues:

Unfortunately, it was obvious we couldn't take the Italians with us, and it was equally obvious they were determined to join us. Captain Spivey lined up the jeeps with the Italian's diesel truck behind and DRs in front and looking like John Wayne, Capt. Spivey stood up in the leading jeep, raised his right arm and shouted 'forward'. We had gone half a mile before the Italians had started, and never saw them again.

Laurence was also part of 2 Platoon which dashed up the coast, and were the first Allies to secure Bari, the port city on the Adriatic coast. The Italian military command quickly surrendered, but the Platoon then had to convince the Italian's there were more soldiers present in the town than there actually were. In their book, *Leading the Way to Arnhem*, the authors described how 2 Platoon drove and marched around the town in a variety of guises. Battledress with berets, then steel helmets, airborne smocks, denims, with and without equipment, until the local population must have become convinced there were more troops present than in reality. Laurence, with his sense of humour, would have enjoyed the light relief that this brought.

Bari, Italy, November 1943. Laurence second from left.
(By permission of the Metropolitan Police Museum)

The Pathfinder's mission had been successful, and Laurence's Italian job was coming to an end. They had performed their tasks exceptionally well and as they travelled back to Taranto; they had news which caused a wave of excitement through the men, the possibility that they may be returning to England to train for the second front: the invasion of German occupied France.

4

UP THE ATLAS IN ALGERIA

Just like they'd arrived, the pathfinders left Taranto on the 19 November 1943, by ship. Laurence wrote about what happened:

> We left in a French merchant ship the SS *Cuba*. We joined a Mediterranean convoy and in a short time the ship's engines failed; there was a strong rumour going the rounds that it was sabotage. We left the convoy and docked at Augusta. Although we had been officially informed that we were going to a new theatre of operations, it was now the unanimous verdict of us all that we were returning to England for the second front. The expectation was overwhelming. We stayed in Augusta for a couple of days and as we could not find another convoy, we returned to North Africa to our undying disappointment.

Although hoping they may be going back to Britain, the company instead travelled to a tented military camp in Blida, northern Algeria at the base of the Tell Atlas Mountains. The fact it was peaceful after the mission in Italy, may have been gratefully received, but the pathfinders were a trained, motivated fighting unit and Laurence recollects that in fact, 'the boredom at Blida and the disappointment at being there I found most depressing, although the company of our comrades and our good humour saw us through.'

Laurence's written recollections of his time there involved him and his mates, frequently visiting the local French/Arab cinema–for sobering up after visiting the local taverns. He became famous for creating a 'cocktail' he called a 'Lulu' which had as its base Crème de Menthe, and probably consisted of the addition of any other alcoholic beverage that was locally available.

An incident recalled by his great friend, Fred Weatherly (a fellow

Pathfinder), happened on Christmas Eve 1943, when Fred, Laurence and several other soldiers of the company had spent time imbibing Eau de Vie (fruit brandy) and Crème de Banane in large quantities, causing Fred to pass out on the steps of the cinema. Laurence was seen slapping Fred's face to bring him round by a passing Army Padre who threatened to have Laurence arrested for 'grievous bodily harm', but somehow Fred was carried into the cinema, and woke up to Deanna Durbin singing 'Beneath the lights of Home.'

In later years Laurence wrote, 'At Blida, Old Bob (the nickname of the commanding officer, Major Wilson) and the company sergeant major had a hard task to occupy the troops. In retrospect, I realise how well they catered for our superb fitness.'

One way to keep the company fit and motivated was to use the Atlas Mountains as training. Fred Weatherley's and Laurence's written recollection tells of an incident:

The company was sent in groups to climb the Atlas Mountain. We… (Laurence and Fred, and others)… were first in very quick time–racing up the mountain paths like mountain goats to the top and sliding back down the shale on our heels and backsides. Major Wilson wouldn't believe we had been to the top and back and sent us up again with orders to bring something back to prove we'd reached the top this time. Naturally we were incensed at this and we set off again at a good lick to prove him wrong.

When we got back with our trophy, Major Wilson was at Division or somewhere and when he returned, he found in front of his tent our little group, several highly agitated locals, a number of amused and interested onlookers, and a mangy looking donkey. The locals were shouting and gesticulating angrily… Major Wilson asked 'What the hell do they want?' There was a long pause then Laurence said 'I think they want their donkey Sir!' Major Wilson went an unattractive shade of purple and threatened us with all sorts of mayhem if we didn't get rid of the donkey and locals, immediately. This we did, placating the locals with a handful of French Francs, and Major Wilson retired to his tent muttering ominously 'I'll see you lot later.' We waited for the axe to fall, but nothing more was heard. I did hear that after several mellowing whiskies in the Mess that evening, Wilson had a good laugh over the whole thing and was heard to say "I'll never get the better of those young b******ds."

Soon, to the pathfinders' and Laurence's great relief, the 'Boredom of Blida' was over, for on Christmas day they finally set sail, heading back to 'Blighty' with their role in the coming second front still unknown. They arrived back in England and carried on training with new equipment and exercises.

Finally, Operation Overlord was launched on 6 June 1944: D-Day. It was the invasion of German occupied France that the pathfinders had hoped they would be involved with, but to their great disappointment it was not to be. Highly trained and raring to go, the men's frustrations must have been boiling over. Then, after two months of just reading about the Allies advance into occupied Europe, Laurence, finally got his chance to become involved. He was about to play an essential, leading part in one of the most famous, greatest and ill-fated airborne operations in history: Operation Market Garden–the Battle of Arnhem.

5

A BIG CHEER WENT UP

'I was actually relieved to be going because we'd been waiting months to go. We'd had 16 operations all cancelled at the last minute. A big cheer went up when we knew we were going,' Laurence explained in an interview to the Barnet Press in 2004, and it reveals his, and the other pathfinders', attitude in needing to make a contribution to ending the war. All were highly trained and motivated soldiers, and literally fighting fit.

Coincidentally, like when he first joined the army in 1940 in the Dorsetshire Regiment, Laurence was again under the ultimate command of the now General Montgomery, for Operation Market Garden was Monty's plan. Monty wanted to shorten the war, and the plan was a high-risk operation for the Allies to secure the bridges across the River Rhine and enable an advance into the north of Germany. The US 101st and 82nd Airborne Divisions were to capture Grave, Veghel, Eindhoven, and Nijmegen bridges, leaving the British 1st Airborne Division and the 1st Polish Independent Parachute Brigade, to capture the furthest bridge at Arnhem. The British 30 Corps, an armoured division, was to make its way through Belgium in time to meet the British & Polish, secure Arnhem bridge and liberate the Netherlands.

A vast Armada of aircraft and gliders containing paratroopers, weapons, vehicles and supplies were to take off from all over England. To succeed, they needed to be guided in to where to drop the paratroopers and land the gliders when they got to the Netherlands, and for this they needed an advanced unit. At last, their 'finest hour' had arrived: Laurence and the pathfinders were to be first in to the battle.

On 17 September 1944, on a crisp sunny morning, along with over 180 officers and men in full battledress, weaponry and equipment,

Laurence arrived at the RAF Fairford airfield in Gloucestershire. He noticed the air crew preparing the twelve large Stirling bombers lined up on the runway, in readiness to fly them over the North Sea to the Netherlands. What was going through Laurence's mind when he climbed into the aircraft, knowing his was going to jump into a country occupied by the enemy? 'We weren't scared when we jumped out. We had a job to do,' he explained. He'd already been given his tasks as a member of 2 Platoon: to mark out the DZs and LZs for the thousands of soldiers and hundreds of gliders who were in the following 'Airborne Armada'. These zones were to be marked out on several large, flat fields near Wolfheze, west of the town of Arnhem.

As the pathfinders jumped out, there was little German opposition, in fact the German's were completely taken by surprise. Laurence explained, 'When we landed, we captured fifteen Germans who were peacefully having their Sunday picnic in the fields.' After successfully marking out the Zones, the following Armada came into view, and the sight was truly incredible. As Laurence observed when the vast number of planes and gliders came towards him, 'It seemed a bit unreal, seemed never ending. It must have been about a hundred miles long. It must have been a terrific sight for the Dutch.'

Over the following days, around 10,000 soldiers arrived by parachute and glider and initially, the drop and landings went well. The pathfinders had done their job. But very soon things started to go wrong. 'The radios were useless. It's quite amazing: the Germans could ring us up and listen to us so they had all the information about what we were doing.' Laurence told the Barnet Press in 2004.

He was beginning to realise that he'd need to use all the military training he'd had, his survival skills learned growing up on the tough streets of London, and rely on the camaraderie and competence of his fellow pathfinders, if he was going to get out alive.

Laurence described what happened in interviews with his daughter:

We went out on patrol on the second day. We had to find out where the Germans were. We were stationed in a big farmhouse where Company HQ was inside. Of course, the radio sets were useless and this caused a lot of damage. We came back from the patrol and of course no one could tell us the Germans had rushed the HQ and our lot had gone... as we approached, we heard a half-track start up and then a couple of machine-guns opened fire, so I ran to the house with my brilliant British Sten gun and saw a German. I thought it was a postman at first–he had a big bag of grenades which he started chucking at me, but they didn't go off and I pressed my trigger and nothing happened. I went round the side of the house, put in a new magazine and went back and nothing–the gun wouldn't work, marvellous! So, I dashed across the grounds of the house and got into a sort of sandpit there and then heard Jim Stewart and Johnny Stanleigh shouting, so Jim–a very brave soldier indeed–said 'we'll give you covering fire'. I flew over a fence to get away and I thought it was about eight feet but when we went back after the war, it was actually only about four foot!

The pathfinders were lightly armed and what hadn't been planned for was the extent of the German Army's equipment and the presence of parts of two SS Panzer (tank) divisions. Laurence talked many times of how a tank was firing at his platoon, pinning them down, on a road near the Ommershof–a large house and estate. One of Laurence's platoon, Louis Landon, a German Jewish refugee, decided to try and destroy it. Taking his PIAT (Projector, Infantry, Anti-Tank) gun with him, and laying down near the road, he fired successfully stopping the tank, but he was shot as he moved away and later died of his wounds. This upset Laurence very deeply, and he always spoke of Louis. 'Louis was a Berliner, one of nature's gentlemen and a good soldier. He taught me how to play chess.'

For the first few days, Laurence and the pathfinders were fighting in woods that covered the area between the landing site and Arnhem. As the fierce fighting continued, most of the supplies that were being dropped by the RAF failed to reach the Allies, and as the enemy closed in, the pathfinders, and other soldiers of the division, were pushed towards a town called Oosterbeek, which was west of Arnhem. Oosterbeek had a crossroads at its centre, and Laurence's platoon had to take over some of the houses in Pietersbergseweg: one of the roads leading off the crossroads. The soldiers were being attacked relentlessly, and had to form a defensive ring round the town, called the Oosterbeek Perimeter.

The Dutch houses from which Laurence and the pathfinders were defending, were large with sturdy walls and provided some protection, but now Laurence was involved in urban warfare: the most difficult type of fighting. It was close combat, house-to-house fighting, with Dutch civilian families sheltering in the basements of their houses as the enemy's tanks and self-propelled guns started moving closer, shelling the Airborne soldiers. Nowhere was safe.

Laurence told of how answering 'a call of nature' nearly cost him his life:

> When I went outside to relieve myself, you always go by a tree, a bit of camouflage. I don't know whether they could see me, I don't know whether it was a tank but it had a gun and machine gun… it was gardens I had to run across and by the time they got the machine guns going, I'd gone. I could hear it behind me… I ran… into the back door and up the stairs and they saw me and fired the machine gun. Shortly after, we had a shell in the front room, it came in the back wall and out the front room. I was concussed by this shell. As I regained consciousness I could see white stuff, and I thought that's a bit of luck: I'm in heaven!

The 'white stuff' was probably the insides of soft furnishings, like mattresses, the men had used to barricade the walls and doors.

As days of heavy fighting continued in Oosterbeek, the medical staff at the military dressing stations, who were treating the ever-increasing wounded, were struggling to cope. They were receiving both British and German injured, and on 24 September a negotiated ceasefire was agreed to evacuate the wounded. In complete silence, and under armed guard, there was a procession of wounded British and German soldiers; some were carried on stretchers and others who were able to walk, were helped by their comrades. Laurence watched as they slowly passed by the house he was defending, noticing how the German medics used brown paper bandages, instead of proper dressings. He saw some of his fellow pathfinders in the procession, 'We saw Alan Sharman walking slowly past our house, head bowed and with a thin blanket wrapped round his shoulders. I wasn't aware at the time that he'd been wounded. It seemed as if we could have stretched out an arm and touched him, but we did not move or speak for fear of compromising the truce.'

After the evacuation, fierce fighting started up again. This time the German soldiers were going house to house. 'We were losing men all over the place. The Germans had flame throwers. It was ridiculous and we had no chance against those tanks. We lost a third of our men,' Laurence told the Barnet Press.

The houses from which Laurence was fighting, Oosterbeek.
(Jan Scott)

As the days went on, the situation of the men was desperate and the pathfinders were running out of ammunition: Laurence was using a German rifle, and food and other essential supplies were scarce or non-existent, but the soldiers kept fighting to keep the Oosterbeek Perimeter secure in the hope that 30 Corps would still reach them. Unfortunately, the armoured division never did: having reached Nijmegen after coming under horrendously heavy enemy fire, their route became known as 'Hell's Highway'.

If all the men fighting in Oosterbeek were not going to be killed or captured, something had to be done and fast. It was: Operation Berlin became the name of the evacuation of the remainder of the 1st Airborne Division and the Polish. It was to take place at night and ferry all the men across the River Rhine in small boats steered by Canadian engineers.

For Laurence, and the other pathfinders in the house on Pietersbergsweg, the message came through that they had to make their way down to the river, guided by a line of white ribbon, to Oosterbeek Church, and then pass along the river bank to the boats.

It was the wet, windy night of 25 September, and Laurence recounted what happened:

We were still were fighting in our last house in Oosterbeek village when we were told that we were to retreat. The house belonged to a Dutch dentist. It was a mess and some of his family were hiding in the cellar. We used to throw in sweets and stuff when we could. All the time we had heavy mortar and artillery barrage firing at us–it was all noise.

We were told to withdraw across the river at 10 pm and when we knew, we went round telling the Dutch civilians. We didn't want to go and leave them behind. We were resigned to fighting to the end and to being killed. I felt so angry. It seemed such a waste. Nine days of fighting and all those people killed and wounded and we had to leave the Dutch people behind, I felt guilty. We wanted to stay.

We formed up outside on the grassland of the village… in platoons and it was pitch black and pouring with rain. We'd cut up bits of blankets and tied them over our boots and bayonets–sort of fastened them somehow so they wouldn't jingle. The tail at the back of our camouflage smocks was loose and as it was pitch black, we had to hold each other's smock tails as we walked together. Some soldiers were so tired they just sat down and went to sleep. I could see their shadows on the ground.

We were supposed to move off together and leave with 1 Platoon but it was so dark we somehow separated and were left behind. 1 Platoon had just moved off before us. In hindsight it was lucky we were separated as 1 Platoon ran into a machine gun ambush and some were killed and wounded. Our commanding officer, Major Bob Wilson, was hit by a bullet that scraped the bridge of his nose and knocked him out.

We knew before we moved off that the British artillery over the Rhine was firing Very lights, like flares, showing where we had to aim for. They were from two points on the far bank, half a mile apart, so we knew we were walking towards where the boats were going to get us across. The German's were firing mortar bombs at us, thinking more of the British were coming over the river, not withdrawing.

In the dark and rain, four of us got separated from the others in the Platoon, Snowy Wheatley, Fred Weatherly, Lol Colbrooke and me. We huddled together in the woods by the river bank. I had my emergency ration of a tin with a heavy bar of chocolate in it, so we had some chocolate each and drank the rain. All the time there were people shuffling past us and the German's mortaring us. We were dead tired but carried on plodding along past shadows of bodies on the ground, some were dead, some fell asleep and missed the boats. We passed Oosterbeek church and the angel's house–Kate ter Horst's house–and finally came along the tail end of a long queue, the men at the front were standing in the water. Suddenly loads of them rushed from the back to the front and into the water, panicking to get into the boats that came in. Us four held back, thinking no way were we going to get over the river here.

We decided to walk down the river bank, thinking we would have to swim across. Then one of these little boats appeared out of nowhere. There was no noise, it just drifted towards us. It had broken down, and just drifted into the bank right by us. We couldn't see who was in it but we climbed in. The Canadian Engineer got the engine going but it failed again about half way across. We were supposed to have got rid of our firearms. I didn't. I kept mine which was actually a German rifle I'd found. Luckily, I did, because I started to paddle the boat with it and we got across the river.

I don't remember many being there to meet us, just heard one of the Canadians say "go over that way," so I followed the way the Canadians told me to go. In the pitch black, somehow, I found myself alone and it was so dark I fell into a shell hole. I kept falling into shell craters, climbing out then falling into another until I got to a road. One of the British soldiers was there and said "not far now. Just walk up the road." It seemed like miles, but I just kept trudging along. I still had blankets on my boots but was too tired to stop and take them off.

As I walked, British soldiers would step out of the darkness, point and say, "not far now". One of them gave me a cigarette. Finally, I saw a small tent. I thought I was hallucinating, but as I got nearer, I realised it was real. Medical Corps were in there and they gave me a cigarette and small drink of rum or brandy. Transport arrived to Elst, then Nijmegen, which was held by the

US Army. It was light by then and I was led into a school, given a bed and left to sleep.

The next day I went to the cookhouse and queued for tea. I found some of the 21st and we stayed together, then we saw our commanding officer, 'Old Bob', Major Wilson at the end of the queue. We all cheered because he'd survived, though he had a plaster over his nose where the bullet had hit him when he was ambushed.

Later that day we left for Belgium in the TCVs and got shelled some of the way. We passed the British tanks and they'd really taken a hammering. Tanks and dead bodies were strewn everywhere, I couldn't help thinking what a waste! We got back to England in US Dakotas. We weren't relieved to get back, because of all those we'd left behind, the Dutch people and our friends. It was when we got back that we found out who was missing from the company.

Back in London, for Laurence's mum, dad and sister, it must have been a terribly worrying time. The newspapers had covered the battle with daily accounts and the family would have known that the situation for the soldiers was desperate and that hundreds of men had been killed with only 2,000 or so having made it to safety. When a knock had come at the family's door and Emma saw the uniformed telegram boy standing on the step, her heart must have skipped a beat, fearing the worst had happened to Laurence. However, instead there were tears of relief when she read that he'd, safely, made it back to England. Forgetting to close the door, and with the telegram in hand, she ran out into the road. A car screeched to a halt, just avoiding knocking Emma over. She uttered an apology and carried on running to Morris', nearby, work place to tell him the good news. It must have been a joyous moment for the family.

Laurence came out of the battle with mixed feelings: he'd survived when many of his fellow pathfinders had been killed, including many friends. In military speak the 'casualties were light' considering the pathfinders went in first, which was a testament to their ability to fight and survive adversity. Many were experienced soldiers, and several were Jewish refugees from Germany, Poland and Austria, who could speak German, and maybe being able to understand the enemy helped the company's survival.

Whenever Laurence spoke about Arnhem, it was with a mixture of guilt, sorrow and pride. He was always amazed by the support of the Dutch people, but he always felt guilty for taking over their houses, which in turn, made them a target for the enemy, and caused the civilians to have to flee their homes. He felt guilty for leaving them behind too, when the soldiers had to retreat across the river. He'd always get tearful when he talked about the Dutch families, 'They were hiding in the cellars, and we'd throw down sweets and food to them when we could. I felt awful about leaving them and what happened after we left.' The Dutch were forced to leave Oosterbeek and Arnhem by the Germans, as a reprisal for 'collaborating' with the airborne soldiers, and they wouldn't return to their homes until after 5 May 1945, when the Netherlands were finally liberated.

An explanation as to why the Dutch were so supportive of the 'Airbornes' as they called them, was given to the author by Ans Kramer. She had lived with her family in one of the houses the pathfinder's 1 Platoon had occupied, at 8 Stationsweg. Ans explained how terrible it had been living under occupation. The family had a secret radio set, even though the Germans had banned the possession of radios. The family would listen in secret to the broadcasts from the BBC of Radio Oranje: a programme providing information to the Dutch people and also coded messages for the Dutch Resistance. Ans remembered how her mother had shouted at her because she was humming the tune from the radio. If the enemy heard her, they would have realised the family had a radio and they could have been shot.

Ans explained that, 'After years of living in fear, the 'Airbornes' had come from the sky, and fought and died for our freedom, in our homes and gardens. We realised we were not forgotten. They gave us hope.'

6

PEACE AND PEGGY

Laurence and the pathfinders returned from fighting in what was, unknown to them at the time, to become one of the most famous battles of the war. They flew back to Newark, a town in Nottinghamshire, where they had been stationed before they left for Arnhem, and resumed training for another Airborne operation if needed, but that operation never came.

However, life as it does, changed in a split second and for Laurence, on one of his periods of leave back in 'smoky old' London, he met the love of his life, Peggy. For the teenage Peggy, the war had involved long shifts doing war work at the Standard Telephone Company in North London, great friendships and the excitement of living in a city, where lots of young men from all over the world, were milling around pubs and clubs. It was to be in a North London pub where she met a young, fit, lean man in uniform, back from fighting at Arnhem. He flashed his winning smile, went up to her and asked the very romantic question, 'Can you hold my pint of beer while I go to the toilet.' Peggy said, 'Yes', and from then on, they were inseparable. When and where Laurence proposed marriage isn't known, but their time together was to be brief as Laurence had yet another mission.

On 8 May 1945, the German armed forces surrendered unconditionally to the Allies and the war in Europe was over. However, whilst Laurence's family, Peggy and her friends celebrated VE Day, dancing and flag waving outside Buckingham Palace, Laurence and the pathfinders were preparing to be flown to Norway to assist with the German surrender. The Germans had occupied Norway from April 1940 and after Arnhem, when Laurence and the pathfinders had fought for their lives, it must have been some sort of compensation and satisfaction to be involved in the round up of the defeated enemy.

Laurence explained what happened in his written recollection *A Norwegian Saga*, 'On VE Day plus 1, the Company flew to Norway to take part in the roundup of around 365,000 German troops whose commanders had not surrendered unconditionally. With typical British understanding, about 3,000 Airborne troops were sent to carry out this operation.'

Arriving at Stavanger Airport with 2 Platoon, then billeted at Honefoss, Laurence was involved in searching for members of the Gestapo and SS (Schutzstaffel), many of whom were 'hiding in plain sight' and dressed in normal German Army uniforms or civilian clothing. The Norwegians, who had been held in a concentration camp called Grini, helped identify those Gestapo and SS, who were then taken by the military police to stand trial for war crimes. Laurence explained, 'We had no trouble at all... Every action was carried out without violence. After we had got them all confined, we stayed in Norway until August 1945.'

It must have been a relief that there was no danger for the men, and they even had time to relax in the beautiful countryside and enjoy the pleasures of victory. Laurence told of an event which certainly helped him celebrate:

We received a complaint from the (German) Surgeon General, that Norwegians were stopping a truck containing medical supplies for the German Prisoners of War, and confiscating some of them. Our interpreter was ordered to accompany the truck when it picked up supplies and bring it to our billet so that the contents could be examined. When the truck arrived, it was found to contain Three Star Hennessey, Black and White Scotch, Johnny Walker Scotch, a variety of British and French beers, popular brands of cigarettes etc. and an up-market quantity of caviar. This was loot brought from France after the German retreat from Caen. We were meticulously fair: we only kept half!

Even though the pathfinders found time to relax, Laurence was still on active duty and far away from his family, and Peggy. Getting home was beginning to become the focus of his mind. In London, the area surrounding Central Street, where his family lived had been decimated by bombing during The Blitz. They were all incredibly lucky to have escaped unharmed. Laurence's great relief that they had all miraculously survived the war, and his longing to be back with his family for good, was evident in this reply he sent to his parents' letter, which had reached him in Norway, he wrote:

Cpl. L. Solomon.
21st Ind. Para. Coy.

Sunday
29.7.45

Dear Mum & Dad,
Your letter has heartened me so much, Mum, knowing you are going away for a few days. I don't have to tell you how much I love you, Mum, you have always known. If anything ever happened to you I could never live. In a few days' time you will hear from Danny & then you will feel different. I shall definitely be home soon and then we can rejoice. Ramsgate is very nice and you will enjoy your stay there very much.

Remember Bill Smith and myself cycled there for our holiday just before the war? I shan't forget because on the first two days we were blistered by the sun and we didn't have any sleep for the rest of our stay. Don't forget to take plenty of sun-burn lotion with you when you go. I want to see you nice and tanned when I come home, not looking like a tomato.

You will find plenty to do there if it is anything like pre-war days. I don't think it has been touched much by the war. Don't forget to send me a bit of Ramsgate rock, seems ages since I have had any.

I have received all your cigarettes, Mum, I thought it was more than five you sent.

We are tolerating our stay in Norway now that we know we shall be returning to Blighty very soon. We saw a film last Wednesday called *The Keys of the Kingdom* and we enjoyed it very much. There were one or two minor faults though. The screen appeared as if it was raining all the time and the film kept breaking down every quarter of an hour, but it was a film and we appreciated it as such.

Give my love to my beautiful sister.
Best of luck and love,
From your loving son, Laurie

***

Thankfully, after returning from Norway, Laurence had leave to see his family and Peggy before his next posting. He'd brought Peggy a gift of a necklace back from Norway. It was inscribed 'To Peg, all my love Laurie' and she wore this necklace for the rest of her life.

But active duty was still ongoing and Laurence and the pathfinders, still had another task, this time it was in the Middle East and the British Mandate for Palestine. As part of the 6th Airborne Division, Laurence arrived at Haifa in November 1945, to help 'police' the ever increasingly complicated situation that existed there. Suffice to say, after surviving Arnhem, he didn't want to get shot there and just wanted to get back to civilian life. Finally, to his great relief, in 1946, home beckoned and Laurence arrived back in Blighty to be de-mobilised.

It must have felt strange in many ways: he'd spent six years in the army, spending four of those with the 21st Independent Parachute Company, and experienced a traumatic and intense time with that company, now the day had arrived when they were all to go their separate ways. Laurence swapped his army uniform, for a War Office 'de-mob suit' which was provided by the government for returning soldiers. One very important thing he did before he returned his uniform, was to carefully unpick the stitching of his Parachute Wings, which he'd proudly sewn on four years before, and carefully tucked them into his wallet. They were a symbol of pride and maybe even protection in some way for, miraculously, he had survived one of the most intense battles of the war.

At the military dispersal office, Laurence had to fill in a Soldier's Release Book. With an ink pen, Laurence wrote in his name as 'Laurence Solomon', his rank as 'W/Cpl', his unit as '21 IND. PARA.COY', his regiment as 'A.A.C.' and the date of calling up for military service as '20.6.1940'. His soldier's release leave certificate states 'the above-named man proceeded on release leave on the date shown in the military dispersal unit stamp opposite.' The stamp reads, '22 June 1946 Aldershot'. Almost six years to the day he joined up, he was now officially a civilian. The pathfinders, the 21st Independent Parachute Company, in which he'd so bravely fought, and which had provided such an important role during the war, was disbanded three months later on the 13 September.

After officially being released from active duty, wearing his new 'demob suit', Laurence caught the train back to London, and home to the relief of his family. His brothers, Mark and Danny had also survived the war. As family life in their rented house in Central Street started to be rebuilt amongst the bombed ruins of London, Laurence realised that for him, at last, the war was truly over.

7

A DIFFERENT UNIFORM

Not only was the bomb-damaged City of London completely different from the one in which he'd grown up, so was post-war Britain. Laurence had supported Winston Churchill as a great war leader, but he was pleased that now there was a Labour Government. Clement Attlee was Prime Minister and the welfare state was created to include a new National Health Service, and changes to the policing of London were occurring with the Metropolitan Police area being expanded, along with a new Police Training School Division.

Laurence now had two new missions ahead: to find a new job and, with great excitement, become Peggy's husband. Peggy, her full name being Margaret Janette Amelia Sharman, was born in on 13 January 1926, in Stroud Green, a leafy suburb of North London. She'd had a challenging childhood, as her birth mother had left the family when Peggy was just three-years-old, and she was brought up mostly by her Gran: her dad's mother. Her father, John, was an infantry veteran of the First World War. He'd married again, to Lilian, and trained in the highly skilled job of a steam train fireman, and later became a train driver.

Peggy worked hard at school, but as she reached the age of thirteen the Second World War had started and as soon as she was old enough, she was employed in war work at, the then, Standard Telephones and Cables Factory (STC) in New Southgate, North London. She described her work:

It was long hours standing all day. From 7.30 in the morning to 6.30 in the evening, five days a week, and we worked Saturday mornings as well. I was a paint-sprayer standing under a hood with waterfalls going down the back to take the spray and dust away. I was spraying radio components, but we weren't told what they actually were.

The STC factory was situated by a major railway line leading into central London. It was the same line on which John, Peggy's father, worked. The railway line and factory were easy to spot from the air and were often targeted by enemy bombers. Peggy explained what happened in those raids:

> They told us there was an air-raid, so we went to the shelters nearby. Dank, dark places, with big passages that were interconnected. They had lights though, and we sat on benches along the walls. We could still hear the bombers flying overhead, then I heard the explosions. When they gave the all-clear we came back up and had to leave our names and addresses at the gate before we went home. The next day we were back at work.

In June 1944, the first German V-1 flying bomb, or 'doodlebug' as they were called, hit London and in August 1944, one landed on the factory where Peggy worked. Luckily, she wasn't on her shift at the time, but her father didn't know this. She later heard that he'd stopped his train engine, got out and walked up the railway line to the factory to try and find her.

Meeting Laurence had also started a new chapter for Peggy and she was much loved by Laurence's family. She'd accepted Laurence's proposal of marriage, but they couldn't afford an engagement ring, even so that didn't dampen the sheer joy of them both meeting, and being able to marry. They were truly 'soul-mates.'

Laurence and Peggy's wedding. Front: Rae, Emma, Laurence, Peggy, John,
Lilian Back: Morris, unknown, Joyce.
(A. M. Davis and Jan Scott)

Their modest wedding was held at Edmonton Registry Office on 12
October 1946, with Laurence in his de-mob suit and Peggy, in a suit
of two-toned green–her favourite colour–that her friend, Joyce, had
made. Morris, Emma and Rae attended the wedding for the groom,
and John, Lilian and Peggy's great friend Joyce, attended for the bride.
The war years had been a gruelling time for both families, but
somehow, they'd all come through, dressed up in the best clothes they
had at the time, and celebrated the beginning of a new chapter for all
of them. Laurence then moved into Park Ridings, near Wood Green,
North London, where Peggy lived with her family.

After the personally testing situation of being in an elite army unit,
a return to his pre-war trade of a printing press operator, was never
going to be Laurence's ideal job. But what was the perfect job for him?
One that was physical, and used his sharp intellect, after all he was still
a young fit man of twenty-six. When he'd come back from Arnhem,
he'd visited the parents of a friend who had been killed there, and they
had told him their son had wanted to join the police after the war.

Maybe it was a way of fulfilling his friends wish, and a tribute to him, as well as needing a steady career, because on 16 September 1946, Laurence arrived at the Metropolitan Police Training School in Hendon. He picked up an ink pen, signed his name on a ledger, got his warrant number and a new uniform, and the day before Christmas eve in 1946, he was assigned to 'Y' division, Hornsey Police Station in North London. He was now a Trainee Police Constable.

Laurence joins the Met.
(By permission of the Metropolitan Police Museum)

Being a trainee and a constable in 1946 meant learning the law at training school, shift work: early, late and night shifts, walking a beat, using a whistle, a wooden truncheon, handcuffs, and using navy-blue police phone boxes which were stationed in the streets. Laurence had to 'ring in' to the police station and report where he was and details of any crimes. It was a very physical job and enabled Laurence to stay fit, and use his natural athleticism and running ability when enthusiastically chasing after criminals.

Metropolitan Police Training School, 1946. Laurence is second row, fourth from left.
(T. H. Everitt & Son. By permission of the Metropolitan Police Museum)

At home, the couple settled into married life and Peggy carried on working until 1950, when they had their first child, a son. The same year, Laurence did something similar as his dad Morris had done in the First World War: he changed his surname from Solomon to Scott, but permanently. It was his personal choice, but he'd kept his surname as Solomon in the Army and was known as 'Solly' to his Army mates. During the war, the European Jewish refugees who fought alongside Laurence with the pathfinders, were told to change their names to a British one in case they were captured. If Laurence had been captured, having an identifiably Jewish surname, he would probably have been shot or sent to a concentration camp.

Laurence took to police work like a 'duck to water' as the saying goes. His ability to catch criminals started to become recognised by the senior management of the Metropolitan Police and Laurence started to get commendations for bravery. These commendations were for arresting thieves, when Laurence was both on and off duty, and were a prelude to what was to come. Unknown to him, a few years later, like at Arnhem, he would, again, stare death in the face and his bravery would be tested to its limits.

Although Laurence loved the job, he felt it was time for a change: he wanted to get out of uniform and working outside in all weathers, and into the sharp suits of the detectives. He also, more importantly, needed the mental challenge that detective work required. So, he applied for and was accepted for detective training school, and in late 1952 he became Detective Constable Scott. His first attachment to the CID (Criminal Investigation Department) was in Bow Street Station, famous as the place where the 'Bow Street Runners' started and opposite Covent Garden Opera House.

As Laurence settled into being a detective, on the home front, in 1955, the family finally moved into a large house in Southgate, North London. It was rented from the Police, who at that time owned several properties for families to rent. It must have been lovely to have space, and Peggy made firm friends with the neighbours, who were also Police families.

Laurence spent the next few years clocking up experience as a detective constable, and a couple of years later, in 1957, he moved to back to 'Y' Division and Wood Green Police station where he stayed until 1959, when two momentous events happened. The good news was, that now an experienced detective constable, he decided to take his police sergeant exams and was promoted to detective sergeant. He was now advising and managing other police officers, as well as leading investigations. But, sadly, on 11 November–poignantly the official day of remembrance–his beloved sister, Rae, passed away from Multiple Sclerosis aged just thirty-two. She'd had two children, a boy and a girl. It was a devasting blow to the family. Over the years, Laurence would keep her memory alive and would always mention 'Auntie Rae' in conversations for the rest of his life.

Metropolitan Police Detective Training School, March 1963. Laurence is second row, fourth from left.
(T. H. Everitt & Son. By permission of the Metropolitan Police Museum)

Now, as a detective sergeant, Laurence was posted back into Central London, to the CID of Old Street Station. This must have been difficult for Peggy, as longer travelling time to the station and back, coupled with his long working hours, meant she would see even less of her husband. It was to be three years until Laurence was re-assigned back to 'Y' Division, and settled into the busy station at Wood Green, which, to Peggy's relief, was only twenty minutes or so drive from their house. Being a detective was a stressful job, no doubt about that, as Laurence worked on serious crime and murder cases, but it suited his sociable personality. His time was spent going out early morning to make arrests, interviewing criminals whilst puffing on his pipe–for he was a pipe smoker then–taking witness statements, and typing it all up on paper forms which had messy blue carbon copying paper between them. There were no computers in those days and he typed only with his index fingers, but he was fast!

Laurence was still working from Wood Green Station in 1964, when the 'swinging sixties' in London were in their heyday and the city was the centre for fashion. For Laurence and the other CID detectives, sharp, tailored suits and ties were standard attire, and Laurence's tall, lean frame meant his suits had to be hand made by a tailor called Davidovitch in London's East End.

It was in that year, that two major events would completely change Laurence's, and Peggy's, life. In February, Peggy gave birth to their daughter, Janice. Falling pregnant was quite a surprise, as she was in her late thirties at the time and considered a 'geriatric' mother. She may have had mixed feelings about having another child so late, especially at that time: would she have the energy to bring up another baby? Although Laurence's job meant he worked long hours, he helped when he could, getting up in the middle of the night to warm their daughter's milk in a pan on the gas stove and bottle feeding her. It was a very challenging time for the couple, but Peggy managed to devote herself to being a mum second time around, with support from her friends and family.

The second event that year, occurred to a young criminal, but would consequently change Laurence's life in a way none of the family could ever have imagined. On 18 November 1964, standing in the dock of the Old Bailey (the Central Criminal Court), was a nineteen-year-old career criminal called David Barnard. Having already pleaded guilty to his crime, he stood to hear his sentence. The *Daily Mirror* of 19 November reported on what the judge, Justice Milmo, told him, 'In years you are pathetically young, but you are hardened in crime and a thoroughly dangerous criminal. It is no fault of yours that you are not standing in the dock charged with capital murder.'

We'll never know if Barnard remembered he could have been given the death sentence when he committed his crime by walking into a money lenders office in the Finsbury area of London, asking for a loan. The manager, Stanley Tepper, had refused, probably seeing this young lad as no great threat, but appearances can be deceiving. Barnard had previously bought a revolver and six bullets for £15.

Threatening Tepper, Barnard pulled out his revolver and fired a shot at Tepper, grazing his head. He quickly ran out of the back of the shop; Barnard ran out the front. Tepper was lucky he wasn't killed, and straight away reported it to the police. Barnard was already known to the police and from the description Tepper gave, he was arrested the next day at his home where he lived in Clapton.

Although just nineteen, Barnard had already been to borstal in 1962, after admitting to one hundred and seventy-seven cases of housebreaking and stealing. He pleaded guilty to the assault on Tepper, and possessing a gun, and admitted to more thefts from flats. The *Daily Mirror* continued in its report on what Justice Milmo had told Barnard, 'It has got to be realised that dangerous criminals, young or old who carry guns as you did. Are going to be severely punished.' The Judge sentenced Barnard to twelve-years imprisonment, and he was sent to Wormwood Scrubs, a prison in the borough of Hammersmith and Fulham, West London, far away from 'Y' Division in North London, and Wood Green Police Station, where Laurence was working.

However, Barnard wasn't enjoying prison life very much and secretly, along with other inmates, had been filing away at the bars of a window and making a rope from mailbags he'd been making as part of his prison work. In June 1966, two years from starting his sentence, Barnard along with five others, escaped through the window and climbed down the rope of mailbags. By 9 June, four of the escapees had been caught, but Barnard was still on the run and in two days, had travelled to North London, and was hiding in a house in Green Lanes, a road not far from Wood Green Police Station.

It was the afternoon of a warm summer's day, Saturday 11 June, and Laurence was one of three detectives, the other two being Sergeant Alec Eist and Sergeant Doug Davies, who were sitting in an unmarked police vehicle, watching a house in Green Lanes. There was a car parked outside the house that the officer's knew thieves had been using in a series of house breakings. The detectives decided to investigate. They got out of their vehicle and Sergeant Davies knocked on the front door and talked to a woman who opened it.

Laurence went round the side of the house. He explained, 'I had a hunch, you know, just something wasn't right. I was round the side of the house and looked through the letter box and just saw this bloke come out of a room and cross the passage way. I shouted out I was a Police Officer, but he went back into the room and came out holding a rifle, then he ran out the back door.'

The *London Gazette* of 1967, described what happened next, 'Sergeant Scott kicked the door open and followed him to the end of the garden. Here the man sat on a wall pointing the rifle at Scott and threatening to shoot if he came any nearer.' Laurence, having had many a rifle pointed at him during the war was unfazed, even when Eist recognised the man as the prison escapee Barnard.

Barnard then jumped off the wall, and started running through the back gardens of the terraced houses, with Laurence and Sergeant Eist in pursuit. They ran after Barnard, jumping over garden fences and throwing flower pots at him. If anyone was sitting in their garden that June afternoon, they would have watched in disbelief as an armed criminal ran past them followed by two burly, suited detectives.

The *London Gazette* continues:

> After covering a short distance, the gunman stopped and aimed the rifle at Scott and Eist in turn and threatened to shoot them. He then backed away from the officers still levelling the gun at them.

He ran away again, but Barnard reached the end of the row of gardens and could go no further. The *London Gazette* cites what happened next, Barnard, 'put the rifle to his shoulders, aimed it deliberately at Sergeant Scott who was nearest to him, and said he would shoot if he came any closer. Despite the threats Scott and Eist together closed with the man and with the assistance of Sergeant Davies who joined in the struggle, he was soon disarmed and overpowered.'

When the rifle was seized, it was found to have been loaded with three .22 bullets, and a fourth in the breach ready for firing. Barnard was handcuffed, taken back to the police station and charged. Laurence and the other detectives typed up all the paper work needed for a hearing at the Magistrates Court. Even after all his effort to resist arrest, Barnard pleaded guilty to possessing a firearm with intent to resist arrest, and was sentenced to five years imprisonment on top of the sentence he was already serving.

Laurence had done his duty as a police officer. It was his job, but his bravery, and that of Eist and Davies, had, once again, been noticed. On 2 September 1966, Laurence was highly commended 'for outstanding courage and devotion to duty in tackling and arresting a vicious criminal armed with a loaded firearm.' This time the commendation was from the Commissioner of the Metropolitan Police himself, Sir Joseph Simpson. Then a month later, Laurence was awarded £20 from the Police Reward Fund, the equivalent is £310 today, but proportionally, in 1966 it was a sizeable sum. Enough for a deposit on a house which in 1968 bought the family a semi-detached property in the then, semi-rural London Borough of Barnet.

However, a bigger surprise was coming. It was a usual Saturday for the Scott family on the morning of 11 February 1967: frost on the inside of the windows, coal fires being lit, and the post arriving early in the morning. Laurence picked up a white envelope with the Prime Minister's crest on it, and with extreme puzzlement, opened it to read a letter from one of the Prime Minister's staff which stated that the Queen had approved the Prime Minister's recommendation that the George Medal (GM) be awarded.

Laurence must have been stunned, he was just doing his duty, but he had been awarded the George Medal for conspicuous gallantry, and Laurence found his name listed in 14 February Second Supplement of the *London Gazette* of Friday 10 February for an award. It stated:

> The Queen has been graciously pleased to give orders for the following awards of the George Medal and the British Empire Medal, and for publication in the London Gazette of the names of those specially shown below as having received an expression of Commendation for brave conduct.

> Awarded the George Medal:
> Laurence SCOTT, Sergeant, Metropolitan Police.

The other Sergeants who'd helped make the arrest, Sergeant Alex Eist and Sergeant Doug Davies both, deservedly, received the British Empire Medal.

Laurence was surprised and humbled at the reaction to his award, as letters of congratulations flooded through the letter box at home and on to his desk at Wood Green Station. Roy Jenkins, then Home Secretary, sent a letter just two days after the award was made public. Laurence, always a Labour Party supporter, must have been chuffed to receive it. Jenkins described his actions as gallant and stated how, once being informed of Laurence's bravery, he had informed the Queen leading to Her Majesty awarding the George Medal. He also expressed how Laurence's bravery had been in line with best conduct of the Police Service.

Laurence's George Medal
(Jan Scott)

The Commissioner, Sir Joseph Simpson, hand wrote his letter of congratulations, in which he thanked Laurence for his actions, which had contributed to enhancing the prestige of the police. But Laurence himself, had mixed feelings about getting the award. He told Walter Partington of the *Daily Express*, who interviewed him on 15 February, that he was embarrassed by the award, 'I feel very upset about it. But it is a great honour—one which belongs to my Division of Wood Green which has a lot of brave men in it already.'

Investiture Day was Wednesday 19 July 1967, and it can only be imagined the excitement of Laurence, Peggy, their parents and the family as they arrived outside Buckingham Palace. Laurence looked suave in a hired morning suit, and Peggy looked a treat in her specially made navy blue two- piece, matching shoes and handbag, and a candy pink flowery hat. She beamed with pride, and would always say how the Queen had acknowledged her, before Her Majesty had pinned the medal onto Laurence's suit. In 1967, photography of the ceremony wasn't allowed, so photographs were taken outside the gate, and the press bulbs flashed non-stop for a good while, ensuring the later editions of the newspapers could have a photograph of Laurence proudly holding his medal. A great day, a once in a lifetime experience, was had by all the family.

There is a lovely photograph, taken on the Investiture day, of Morris looking very dapper in his best suit, Laurence in the middle, and Emma in her best two-piece and holding the George Medal. Morris must have been extremely proud of his son. They had a close bond, for both had been soldiers and had fought in wars, and both had been sportsmen: Morris was an army boxer and Laurence, a runner.

Morris, Laurence, and Emma holding Laurence's George Medal
(Jan Scott)

Morris enjoyed six more years, enjoying the visits of his many grandchildren, until on 22 April 1973, he passed away in London's St Bartholomew's hospital. He was eighty-eight years of age. A great age considering he'd spent four years enduring the physical and mental distress as being a prisoner of war. He'd lived a life of resilience and survival, but most importantly of all, he'd lived it with his great love, Emma. Laurence truly was bereft at the loss of his dad.

Laurence spent the rest of his police service working from Wood Green Station, now an experienced and senior detective investigating major crimes. Roy Medcalf was a new detective constable posted to Wood Green in the early 1970s, and gave his opinion of Laurence as his senior detective sergeant. 'Laurie was a great leader and mentor. He always had the best interest of his team at heart and would back them all the way. When the occasion arose, he could be very serious, efficient or compassionate, whatever was required.'

Roy described Laurence as 'a true, old time DS', meaning that Laurence had policed the area for so many years 'he knew the area like the back of his hand and the 'problem' families even better.' It was a way of policing that still relied on extensive local knowledge of, and a productive relationship with, the community on the Police Division. However, Laurence still had his dare-devil, paratrooper side to him. This was famously demonstrated when he asked a colleague he worked with, who owned an Aston Martin Lagonda, to drive it at high speed down the High Street. Laurence stood on the running board, clinging onto the car, waving a truncheon, just like the Keystone Cops in the silent films of the early 1900s. Roy remembered how it was a spectacle 'much to the delight and amazement of the watching public.'

Laurence's time in the police was distinguished by his extraordinary dedication to duty and bravery, his sense of mischief and also compassion in dealing with those he'd arrested. He'd kept a letter from a prisoner in Wormwood Scrubs, who'd thanked him for the kind and fair way he'd been treated when Laurence had arrested him.

He'd been as deeply involved with his family, as he could, spending time with his children, going on family holidays to visit their friend Joyce in Jersey, helping prepare the shellfish for Sunday lunch when his parents came over and spending time encouraging his daughter at school, because she didn't like it much. But the responsibilities of his job were always intervening in family life. One Christmas family night out to see *Aladdin* at a local theatre, the performance was interrupted by Widow Twankey being passed a slip of paper by someone in the wings. In full costume, wig and dress, she sashayed to the front of the stage and read out from the note 'This is a message for someone in the audience. Would a Detective Sergeant Scott please ring Wood Green police station immediately. Thank you!' Laurence, highly embarrassed, apologised to the cast and audience as he got up to find the theatre's phone, and Peggy and Janice had to be driven home, before Laurence went back to the station. The family never saw what happened to Aladdin and Widow Twankey!

All good things must come to an end eventually, and the day came when Laurence had to hand over his handcuffs and warrant card and retire from the police. There is no doubt that being a police officer was exciting, demanding, and at times, dangerous. For Peggy, it had been a great honour that Laurence had been awarded the George Medal, and she was immensely proud of him, but she could have lost her husband that day in 1966 when he was threatened with a loaded rifle. This thought must have played on her mind and caused her anxiety every time he went to work: was he going to come back to her that evening? Laurence's retirement meant the couple could spend more time together, but most of all, for him and Peggy, it meant he was home and safe.

A large leaving party was organised, and Peggy received a big bunch of flowers. Laurence paid tribute to her saying how grateful he was for finding her, and that she'd been very understanding and patient all the way and never complained about the long hours that he had to put in. Being a detective had been the perfect career, and Laurence confirmed this saying, 'if I had to do it all again, I'd probably do the same thing. I've enjoyed it all.'

On his leaving certificate, it states he joined the Metropolitan Police as constable on 16 September 1946 and left on 26 October 1976 as detective sergeant. Underneath is typed 'His conduct was Exemplary'.

8

NOT REALLY RETIRED

Laurence didn't entirely leave the Police, as he immediately took up the civilian staff post of clerk at the CID office at Hornsey Police station, where he'd started as a constable and not far from his old patch of Wood Green. Although no longer a police officer investigating crimes, it was a job of considerable responsibility; ensuring paperwork was completed and ready for court, victims and witnesses were warned for hearings and trials, and Laurence helped with advising investigating officers on cases using his years of experience and expert knowledge.

But not having the stress of being a police officer meant there was room for a bit of the old cheeky Laurence to reappear. He started to refer to himself as 'Ye Olde Clerk'. He would get post delivered to work addressed to 'Ye Olde Clerk, CID YR.' and write letters to the Metropolitan Police Commissioner's on their birthdays' signing them 'Ye Olde Clerk at YR'.

In the beginning of the 1980's, on a visit to Hornsey Station by, the then, Metropolitan Police Commissioner McNee, the Commissioner noticed that Laurence was wearing his Parachute Regiment tie which he always wore to work. He asked him about it, but Laurence refused to tell him until he'd made a donation to the charity box he always kept on his desk. Apologising, the commissioner explained he didn't carry cash. So, Laurence refused to tell him. Finally, one of McNee's staff had to put his money in the box, then Laurence explained to McNee that he fought at Arnhem and showed him his George Medal. It was all done with good humour.

Although Laurence was now working a nine to five job for the first time in his life, it certainly wasn't time to relax, as working for the CID meant he was still involved with and affected by the crimes they were investigating. Laurence was working at Hornsey in 1983, when on a normal chilly day in early February, a plumber was called to a house in

Cranley Gardens, Muswell Hill, North London. It was an ordinary looking large, terraced house in a leafy road, where the residents had been smelling terrible odours from blocked drains, and had complained to the landlord. When the plumber investigated, he was perturbed to find the blockage was bits of cut up bone and flesh, He asked his manager to have a look the next morning, but an attempt to clear the drain had been made overnight by the man who lived in the top flat, his name was Dennis Nilsen. However, some remains were still found lodged in a pipe. The plumbers called the police and they duly identified the remains as human.

Back at Hornsey station, although not directly involved in the investigation of the case, as CID clerk, Laurence would have been involved in the CID discussions of who the victim might be, and what exactly had happened. This was soon to be answered, as the police were waiting for Nilsen when he returned from work that evening. He calmly showed the officers the remains of many of his victims, which were stored all over his flat. The police at Hornsey had found one of the most notorious British serial killers of all time. After he was arrested, Nilsen confessed in the police car to murdering at least twelve men and boys. A harrowing and challenging murder investigation followed, conducted by a team lead by Hornsey based Detective Chief Inspector Peter Jay—it was three years before DNA forensics were first used. Eventually, at the Old Bailey in November 1983, Nilsen was found guilty of six counts of murder and two of attempted murder and sentenced to life imprisonment.

Although he'd witnessed awful scenes during the war and as a murder case detective, even Laurence was shocked at the evidence found in Nilson's flat, and his ability to kill so many people. He became very pre-occupied with the case at the time, and gave his thoughts on seeing Nilsen in custody at Hornsey Station, 'When I saw him, it was hard to believe what he'd done, he was a thin, ordinary looking bloke. He looked like a bank clerk.'

Laurence stayed as the clerk for two more years until, in March 1985, 'proper' retirement beckoned after thirty-nine years in total, working for the police. Laurence's career had come full circle: he'd started as a police constable at Hornsey, and finished there as a clerk. A large leaving party was organised at the police station, and Laurence felt he'd earned his retirement. 'You've got to go sometime—and anyway I've got my old age pension to look forward to', he'd told *The*

Journal in an interview. He'd been modest about receiving his George Medal, saying it had been a great honour, but that it belonged to all the brave police officers on Wood Green Division, and with similar modesty he'd said in the interview, 'although I'm pleased to be getting such a good send off, I would have been quite happy to slip out the back door without any fuss.'

The 'old age' pension may have beckoned but there was to be no stopping Laurence. Although, finally, he and Peggy had more time to see their many friends and do some travelling, over the years Laurence had been keeping in contact with and tracing his old pathfinder comrades. It was in 1975, that a 21st Independent Parachute Company Club had been formed, and Laurence had been working with other members of the company, to ensure the company's history was remembered and that the members kept in touch. Alongside his police career, Laurence had still been on airborne missions.

9

THE PILGRIM PARATROOPER

The Battle of Arnhem started on 17 September 1944 and ended with the retreat over the River Rhine, on the evening of 25 September. Out of around 10,000 men of the British 1st Airborne Division and the 1st Polish Independent Parachute Brigade, around 2,400 soldiers retreated by climbing into small boats operated by Canadian engineers, or by swimming across the river. This left about 7,500 men dead, wounded or captured. It was a costly operation, but has become one of the most famous battles of the Second World War, due to the tenacity and courage of the airborne soldiers. The Battle of Arnhem 75th Anniversary Commemoration was even debated in Parliament on 14 October 2019, led by a speech made by Labour MP Dan Jarvis, he stated:

> From 17 to 26 September each year, we remember the anniversary of the battle of Arnhem–nine days of some of the fiercest fighting witnessed in the second world war, and the largest airborne operation ever conducted. Arnhem would indeed prove to be a bridge too far, but the story of those who fought there is one of immeasurable bravery and unspeakable tragedy. It would come to define our airborne forces, forging an enduring legacy.

As soon as the Dutch people returned to Arnhem and Oosterbeek to re-build their shattered homes, they also set about establishing official commemorations for the battle. On their return they had found hundreds of bodies of soldiers, discovered in buildings, buried in gardens and the surrounding woods, along with about four hundred Dutch civilians that had also, sadly, been killed. The creation of an Airborne Cemetery was initiated: at first with wooden crosses marking the graves, but these were later replaced by the formal headstones of the Commonwealth War Graves Commission. Dutch children were allocated graves to look after, to ensure the men who died so far away from home, were cared for. This led to the children becoming known as the 'flower children.' Children from local schools and visiting schools from other countries, still take part in laying flowers on the graves at the September Commemorations.

The Dutch people were also conscientious in installing many monuments around the area, including one of the first to be built.: the Airborne Monument. This 'needle' still stands opposite the Hartenstein Airborne Museum in Oosterbeek. The first stone was laid on 25 September 1945 by Major General Urquhart who had been the Commander of the 1st Airborne Division. Also, immediately after the war, the airborne soldiers started to return to find graves of friends who had died in the battle, and to meet with the Dutch people who had supported them so bravely. It became known as a Pilgrimage.

Since he'd been de-mobbed in 1946, Laurence had made many pilgrimages to Oosterbeek and Arnhem, alone and with his family, and had also kept in touch with several of the pathfinders. Eventually many of the surviving men had been contacted and traced and in 1975, a committee was formed to officially start the 21st Independent Parachute Company Club. Laurence was a member of the club from the beginning and eventually became the treasurer. Their first meeting in May 1975, was in Newark, where the pathfinders had stayed before Arnhem, and had returned to after the battle. The club's inaugural meeting was featured in the *Newark Advertiser.*

Red Berets are reunited. The first hello in 30 years. Old friendships were renewed and wives met each other for the first time when survivors of the 21st Independent Parachute Company held their first reunion at Newark. The organising committee managed to contact all but five of the men who made up this elite Army unit stationed at Hawton Road Camp before and after Arnhem in 1944. The reunion also marked the formation of an old comrades' association with former officer, David Eastwood, as president, ex-Sergeant Joe Smith as chairman and former CSM Jim Stewart as secretary-treasurer... Their guests were the mayor and mayoress of Newark, Mr and Mrs Richard Lamb and Mr Cyril Pariby who was the mayor of

Newark at the time of Arnhem… The company boasts some personalities: Detective Sergeant Laurie Scott of the Metropolitan Police won the George Medal for attacking an armed raider.

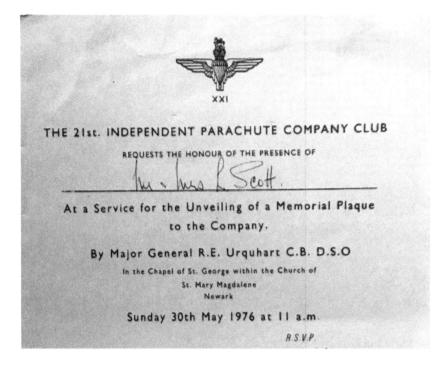

XXI

THE 21st. INDEPENDENT PARACHUTE COMPANY CLUB

REQUESTS THE HONOUR OF THE PRESENCE OF

Mr & Mrs L Scott.

At a Service for the Unveiling of a Memorial Plaque to the Company.

By Major General R.E. Urquhart C.B. D.S.O

In the Chapel of St. George within the Church of

St. Mary Magdalene

Newark

Sunday 30th May 1976 at 11 a.m.

R.S.V.P.

Invitation
(Jan Scott)

These reunions became a high point for Laurence and Peggy in their busy social calendar, and the committee wasted no time in making sure the pathfinders' contribution to the battle was remembered. On 30 May the following year, Peggy and Laurence were invited to the club's event of the unveiling of a wooden memorial plaque in the chapel of St George within the Church of St Mary Magdalene in Newark town. It was unveiled by Major General Urquhart CB DSO, commander of the 1st Airborne Division at Arnhem. The plaque reads 'The 21st Independent Parachute Company left Newark in September 1944 to lead the 1st Airborne Division to Arnhem. Those who survived the battle attended a service in this church and caused this panel to be inscribed in memory of their comrades who did not return'. The plaque became an important focal point for remembrance for Laurence and the men when they attended Sunday morning memorial services at their reunion weekends. The plaque is still there.

Fred Weatherley and Laurence either side of the 21st IPC Plaque, Newark. (Michael Compton, 21st IPC)

Perhaps another point of focus for remembrance was needed in the Netherlands. Even though in Arnhem and Oosterbeek, since 1946, many great monuments to the 'Airbornes' had been built, there wasn't one specifically for the 21st IPC. At a meeting of the club, it was decided there was to be the creation of monument of their own in Oosterbeek. After much deliberation and with the help of the Friends of the Airborne Museum, the site of a grass patch outside the building of Quatre Bras was selected. It was at the intersection of the town's crossroads, where 1 Platoon had held their position as part of the Oosterbeek Perimeter, and opposite to Pietersbergseweg, the road in which Laurence had been fighting in the houses. By 1981, the monument was in position and finished. The unveiling was performed by David Eastwood CBE MC, who was the 1 Platoon Commander and Ans Kramer, the young girl who had lived with her family at 8

Stationsweg, the house that had been occupied by men of 1 Platoon in the battle.

The Newsletter of the Friends of the Airborne Museum, described the unveiling:

> On the 21 September 1981 in the garden of the house 'Quatre bras'… a monument was unveiled to the 21st Independent Parachute Company in memory of their presence in this area in 1944… what is notable in this case is that it concerns an extremely original monument (designed by the 21-year-old Saskia Deurvorst from Oosterbeek) and that the text is, for the first time dedicated to the population of Oosterbeek and the support which was given.

The Dutch had gone through the battle alongside the pathfinders. Where they could, they had provided the men with food, and medical assistance and many had been killed and wounded. Laurence had felt a deep sense of loss and guilt when he had to retreat. After their experiences, Laurence and the club were very concerned to ensure the Dutch citizens were honoured and remembered. The inscription on the monument read, 'In memory of the 21st Independent Parachute Company which held this area during the Battle of Arnhem and of the people of Oosterbeek who sacrificed so much to give their support.'

The monument was made of metal and shaped like the head of a plough, taking its inspiration from the Bible, Isaiah 2:4, 'they shall beat their swords into ploughshares… nation shall not lift up sword against nation, neither shall they learn war anymore.' It gave Laurence and his comrades a focus for their thoughts and grief, especially being directly in the area where they'd fought. The monument still remains an important reminder of the tenacity and bravery of the 21st IPC, in being 'first in' to the battle, their determination in holding their section of the Oosterbeek Perimeter and the close relationships they built with the Dutch people. A bond which holds through the generations.

The 21st IPC, Pathfinder monument, Oosterbeek, 2019.
(Jan Scott)

Within the generations of his own family, Laurence, as the first-born son, had been lucky to have had his mum, Emma, in his life until he'd retired from the police, and Emma had got to know her eleven grand-children. But in November 1986, Laurence's beloved mother passed away peacefully at home aged ninety. She had been devastated at the loss of her husband Morris thirteen years before, but as was the strength of that remarkable generation, she had stoically carried on, and enjoyed regular visits from her ever-expanding family. Laurence would drive down to Radnor Street, EC1, where she still lived in the council flat that she'd lived in with Morris, to visit and bring her back to his house for Sunday dinners.

Emma had lived through tumultuous times and social change. She'd endured terrible anxiety throughout the First World War, waiting for Morris's return from being a prisoner of war in Germany. Then managed to raise a family of four, when finances were limited. She'd witnessed the Suffragette's campaigns in London, which finally gave her the right to vote in 1928, then she'd supported Morris as antisemitism and Fascism rose in the 1930s. Seeing her three sons go off to war must have been heartbreaking, but thankfully they all returned. She'd survived the extensive wartime bombing of London, and endured the loss of her beloved daughter Rae. Even after all this, she was always incredibly kind, liked a giggle, and always wore a hat. Laurence adored his mother, as did the whole family, and her loss was deeply felt.

Laurence and Peggy carried on being involved with the pathfinders club reunions, attending a very special one in October 1996. The couple were surprised with a decorated cake, bunches of flowers and champagne as they celebrated their Golden Wedding Anniversary. Laurence also had a surprise for Peggy: he'd never forgotten that in 1946, they couldn't afford an engagement ring. At last, after fifty years of being married, he finally presented her with a small, solitaire diamond ring.

Even though Laurence was busy helping to organise the 21st Club, he had still kept in contact with his police colleagues and the following year, he was invited to New Scotland Yard, to the dinner of one of his old Wood Green colleagues, Bob Fenton. Bob had invited the ex-commissioner Lord Peter Imbert, and in true Laurence style, like he had to Commissioner McNee, Laurence remarked to Lord Imbert, 'I showed you my George Medal and you didn't give me 50p for charity.' Bob recalled that, 'His Lordship dipped in his pocket and paid up!'

Three years later, a new century began. At the beginning, there was to be more family sadness when in February 2000, Mark, Laurence's brother passed away and in the following year, in June 2001, Danny, Laurence's youngest brother, died. Those close friendships developed through the years, provided support to Laurence and, also, he had a huge event coming up. On 15 September 2004, after an exceptional amount of organising, the men of the 21st Club, their wives, sons and daughters, boarded two coaches for a trip to the 60th Commemoration of the Battle of Arnhem.

Veterans of the pathfinders, Oosterbeek, 2004. Laurence is far right.
(Jan Scott)

The Friday morning, 17 September, was a crisp, clear day, exactly like
the one the pathfinders had back in 1944. In bright sunshine, Laurence
and the 21st IPC Club stood with the large crowd, attending the wreath
laying service at the Airborne Monument in Oosterbeek, and a group
photo was taken with all the men, proudly, standing to attention;
something they never forgot how to do. Laurence and the men, then
lined up round their special Pathfinder Memorial at the crossroads to
remember their friends who had not survived, and also the Dutch
people. More wreaths were laid including one by Ans Kremer, whose
family had always kept in touch, and another by David Eastwood, who
had met Ans as a little girl when he'd fought from the Kremer's house
in Stationsweg.

Pathfinders at their memorial, 2004. Dennis Cramp, Bill Barclay, Harold
Bruce, Joe Smith, Ans Kremer, John Edgar, Don Day, Don Turner,
Laurence.
(Jan Scott)

Later that day, after a group lunch at the Schoonoord Restaurant,
Peggy got a bit upset. It was when Laurence had to leave with some of
the other men, to visit a house in which they'd fought. The other wives,
and Peggy's daughter tried to reassure her he would come back in one
piece, but it was an indication of all the worry she'd had over the years
about him not coming back to her. When Laurence returned that
evening, he'd felt upset too: realising how much Peggy had worried
about his safety over the years and returned from his trip clutching a
red rose which he gave to her. Then they settled down over cakes and
a pot of tea.

Laurence and Peggy visit Oosterbeek, 1980s
(Jan Scott)

That evening, the couple, and their daughter, joined the other pathfinders, to attend the memorial service held near the John Frost (Arnhem) Bridge. They all got seated in the front row, and were very moved to see the Dutch children there, all wearing t-shirts which had printed on them, 'I am a child of freedom, thank you Mr Veteran'. After the wreath laying, Laurence got up to join the veteran's march to a reception at Arnhem Town Hall. Peggy couldn't walk far and was in a wheelchair which her daughter was pushing for her. As they left the area to go to a restaurant, her daughter pushed Peggy into the road where the surface was less bumpy, just as the veterans marched past. As they trundled along, somehow caught up in the march, Peggy started to receive as many cheers as the Arnhem veterans marching with them. Janice remarked to Peggy, 'I think the crowd must think you were a nurse in the battle!', and stuck in the march, they could do nothing except 'go with the flow'. So, thoroughly enjoying the moment, Peggy waved back at the cheering crowds. In many ways she deserved her applause too: for her war-work, surviving the London Blitz, her dedication to supporting her husband in his dangerous job, and helping with fundraising events in the 21st IPC Club.

The Saturday of the weekend was spent at a cold, windy Ginkel Heath. There was a commemorative military parachute drop which thousands of people had come to watch. Wherever they walked, Laurence and the pathfinders were mobbed for autographs and photos like film-stars and Laurence's great friend Don Turner, of 2 Platoon, who'd fought alongside him in the same houses, was interviewed by the BBC.

Laurence, Arnhem 2004
(Jan Scott)

Similarly, the next day, hundreds of people flocked to the crucial Sunday Service of Remembrance at the Airborne Cemetery. It was packed with veterans, their families, serving soldiers from various countries, and the Dutch people. As the service progressed, the moment came when Laurence's favourite hymn, *Abide With Me,* was sung. Sniffles began to be heard throughout the crowd, and along with many others, Laurence pulled his handkerchief from his blazer pocket to wipe tears from his eyes: surrounded by the graves of hundreds of their comrades who had died so young, the airborne veterans' memories flowed back. Then the crowd changed to murmurs of appreciation as, towards the end of the service, the flower children arrived and each child stood by a gravestone. As each child raised their bunches of sunflowers in the air, then carefully placed flowers on each grave, the grateful feelings of everyone present were expressed by clapping which echoed round the cemetery.

Several minutes later, the roar of the engines of Second World War aircraft was heard. Peggy waived enthusiastically as they flew overhead, signalling the end of the service. Laurence's daughter suggested he lay some flowers on his friend, Ben Swallow's, grave. Ben had been a Sergeant of 1 Platoon, but whilst fighting in Ans Kramer's house in Stationsweg, he had been wounded and died at Apeldoorn in December 1944. He was twenty-three. As they got nearer to his grave, tears brimmed up in Laurence's eyes, and he stopped, finding it too emotionally difficult. Maybe he wanted to remember them all as they were before the battle; vibrant, motivated, fit young men. Other members of the 21st IPC Club ensured flowers were placed on the graves of the pathfinders. Then, after much chatting, reminiscing, and a last look at the cemetery, Laurence, Peggy and the rest of the club, clambered into their coaches, and were driven into Oosterbeek for a much-needed lunch.

There was a somewhat rough sea crossing back to England on the ferry the next day, where Peggy and Janice, both pale green with sea sickness, wondered how those who weren't, could still tuck into fish and chips, but it had been a perfect weekend of remembrance for all the 21st IPC Club. As they all disembarked from the coach in London, Janice hailed a black cab for the journey home, and as the driver got out to help with the suitcases, he exclaimed 'Hello Laurie!' Laurence turned and recognised one of his old police chums. More reminiscing, occupied Laurence as they all travelled home.

Laurence and Peggy had thoroughly enjoyed their trip and gratefully so, because at the age of eighty-four, it was to be Laurence's last visit to Oosterbeek and Arnhem: the last time he'd ever see the places, where, sixty years before, he'd parachuted into enemy occupied territory, fought for his life, and managed to escape across the River Rhine on that awful night.

Laurence remained treasurer of the 21st IPC Club, and, along with Peggy, they continued enjoying their hectic social life and involvement, but then, tragically, just before their 61st wedding anniversary, his beloved Peggy passed away suddenly on 5 October 2007. She was eighty-one. Laurence was utterly devastated to lose the love of his life, and he never recovered from his broken heart, but his daughter was living at home and she did her best to look after him, and keep him occupied.

With this aim in mind, Laurence's daughter decided it would be good to visit the Airborne Assault Museum, with which over the years, the 21st IPC Club had kept a close involvement. Laurence hadn't seen it since it had been moved from Aldershot to the Imperial War Museum Duxford site. Laurence polished his shoes, donned his smart navy-blue blazer dressed with his medals and Parachute Regiment Badge, and they drove there to meet the Museum Curator, Jon Baker.

Laurence with Jon Baker, curator of the Airborne Assault Museum, IWM Duxford.
(Jan Scott)

Jon was incredible in the way he engaged Laurence, or 'Solly' as he was known in the army, to talk about his wartime experiences. Jon wrote about his impression of that day:

In 2009 I started work as the curator of Airborne Assault, The Museum of The Parachute Regiment and Airborne Forces. The very first veteran I hosted on a visit was L/Cpl Scott, of the 21st

Independent Pathfinders. Having read something of their history, I was both nervous and in awe of meeting such a gentleman. I needn't have been either, 'Solly', as he told me to call him immediately, was the most gracious, friendly and informative veteran I could have wished to meet. He put me instantly at ease, and was as interested in me as I was with him!

It took a considerable amount of time to walk the kilometre from the guardroom to the museum, as 'Solly' stopped to talk to every group of staff and also, importantly, school children who passed by. Producing his medals from his pocket, he made time for everyone, answering every question with a wit, charm and energy that belied his years.

Sitting with him over lunch, he told me the most remarkable tales of his time with the Pathfinders, from his training to his operational service and his post-war career with the police, and this continued as we viewed the museum. Some of these tales were harrowing, whilst some reduced me to laughter but all were told with an accomplished style and with an eye for detail.

I was genuinely sad when the day ended and 'Solly', accompanied as ever by his daughter Jan, left the site. But sad as that moment was, it also gave me an insight into the minds and experiences of these pioneers of airborne forces. Their dedication, their passion, their quite contemplative bravery, but most importantly the pride that was still so evident in how he carried himself and spoke with others. He remains, in my mind, the most charming and erudite veteran, a man who helped ease me into this daunting job and I miss him.

Laurence never forgot his visit, and always talked about that lovely day.

In the May of that year, Janice helped Laurence pack his suitcase and put on his navy-blue blazer, and drove to his 21st IPC Club reunion at Newark. Even though he was eighty-nine, getting frail and used a walking stick, as soon as he saw his fellow pathfinders, he stood up straighter and walked with purpose. It was the first reunion he'd had without Peggy by his side, but he got through it, led everyone in a sing-song and enjoyed himself. It was to be his last reunion and the final time he'd ever be with his fellow pathfinders at Newark. It had been where, in 1944, they'd paraded in full battle dress, feeling anxious, excited, determined and focussed as they prepared to leave for

Arnhem, and to where they'd returned without a third of their men. Laurence always thought about those young men of the company who never returned, and had an official group photograph of the 21st IPC proudly displayed on the dining room wall. He would always point it out, and talk about the men in it, to every visitor who came to the house.

It was the 65th Anniversary of Arnhem in 2009, and Laurence was too frail to endure the travelling to the commemorations, but one morning a surprise came in the shape of a small parcel in the post. Unwrapping it over breakfast, he found a small metal tie-pin, depicting parachutes over a river and the dates '1944-2009'. Reading the enclosed letter, he was surprised to see that it was from the Mayor of Arnhem's office:

This month marks the 65th anniversary that Operation Market Garden took place in Arnhem and the surrounding area. You were one of those brave parachutists who participated in the airborne landing risking your own life to fight for the liberation of the Netherlands… This commemorative pin is a symbol for the feelings of gratitude, friendship and great respect that the citizens of Arnhem have for the men who took part in Operation Market Garden…We will always appreciate your effort and never forget what your courage meant for the liberation of the Netherlands.

The Arnhem tie pin
(Jan Scott)

'That's nice, that is', Laurence said, in his understated way. He'd appreciated the kind gesture, and that he had been remembered. It cheered him up for weeks. It was another token of appreciation from the Dutch which he treasured. Carefully folding up the letter, and putting it into the small box with the pin, he stored it away next to his George Medal in his bedside drawer.

10

A WARRIOR GOES TO VALHALLA

There was a very unusually long, cold and snowy winter, that year, which delayed spring, but when it came all the flowers erupted from the ground at the same time: snowdrops, daffodils, tulips. Laurence noticed how the pink camellia bush in his garden, which Peggy had loved so much, bloomed with more flowers that it ever had done before. In that glorious spring, on 13 March 2010, Laurence had his ninetieth birthday party. Since Peggy had passed away, he'd constantly worn the blue and green patterned jumper that she'd bought him as a present several Christmases before, and he wore this to his party. It was 'standing room only' until chairs were borrowed from the neighbours as the house became packed with police friends, family, and neighbours. It was a lovely and fun day and everyone tucked into the cake, made with the Parachute Regiment wings on it. So many of his cards had his age on them, and he kept looking at them, saying 'I can't believe I'm ninety!' It was indeed a great age to have reached, and in a way, another great achievement.

Gradually though, throughout the year, Laurence became frailer, until in the early hours of the morning of 31 August 2010, he passed away at home surrounded by photos of his beloved Peggy, his mum and dad, family, friends and that group photograph of the 21st Independent Parachute Company with its pride of place on the wall. It was in black and white, with five rows of young soldiers, and Laurence standing proudly in his red beret in the back row. The photo was taken in March 1944, and some of the men in it would later perish in battle.

As he'd grown frailer, Laurence had gained courage from looking at this photo, thinking about all his friends who had passed away before him and gone to the warrior's resting place known as 'Valhalla.' He was comforted to know they just may all be there waiting to greet him on his arrival.

In battle, in life and in death, they had all forged an unbreakable bond: they were the men he loved, they were his band of brothers.

21st Independent Parachute Company, March 1944
(Panora Ltd and Jan Scott)

11

AFTERLIFE

'We all leave a trial in life, and you Solly, are leaving a great and happy trail.'

This was written by one of Laurence's fellow pathfinders on a card he'd received, just before he passed away. So, what trail did Laurence's extraordinary life and presence leave? Having such a distinguished career in both the army and police, left me, his daughter, with many dilemmas and decisions: where should his final resting place be? What to do with his medals? What should happen to his precious Parachute Wings that I'd found in his bedside drawer?

Laurence had loved both Peggy, and the men he'd fought alongside in Oosterbeek. After much soul searching, and family discussion, it was decided that part of Laurence's ashes were to be buried in a London Cemetery, together with Peggy's, in a rose petal lined grave, and part of his ashes were to be interred in the Arnhem Oosterbeek War Graves Cemetery. There was a tradition of many of the pathfinders wanting to be back with their mates, and with the help of people in the UK and the Netherlands, an official ceremony to bury Laurence's ashes was organised for 16 September 2011. It was agreed that the ashes of Lieutenant David Eastwood CBE MC, would be interred at the same time. David had been the highly regarded commander of 1 Platoon, which had been fighting from houses in Stationsweg, near to the crossroads in Oosterbeek. His bravery earned him a Military Cross for eliminating, and holding off the enemy at the Landing Zone, and for holding the 1 Platoon positions whilst exposed to horrendous enemy attacks.

The ashes of both men were interred behind the grave of John Paul Avallone. John was a Bren gunner in Eastwood's 1 Platoon and on 23 September 1944 was ordered to take up position at the crossroads opposite the Schoonoord Hotel, to eliminate a sniper, but unfortunately his gun jammed and, sadly, he was killed. The interment ceremony was very moving and well attended by both pathfinder's families, friends, the Dutch people, Royal British Legion standard bearers, and Arnhem veteran Johnny Peters, who'd been a member of the 1st Battalion Border Regiment. The service was led by padre Reverend Dr Jeff Cuttell. Now Avallone's grave is the resting place of four pathfinders, as the ashes of Les' Jocky' Morgan, 3 Platoon, were interred there in September 2016.

Laurence and David Eastwood's Interment, 16 September 2011, Arnhem
Oosterbeek War Graves Cemetery
(Berry de Reus berrydereusfotographie.nl)

The next dilemma was what was the best place for my father's medals. They were in a sense public property: the George Medal was a bravery award given by the Government, and Her Majesty, and Laurence's war medals were too, a matter of public interest. There was no point in keeping them hidden away in a safe, they needed to be out there in the world. But I didn't want to donate them as they were valuable. After making a few enquiries I made a hard decision to sell them through a reputable London auctioneer. On a cold day in February 2012, I packed the medals and a box of letters and newspaper cuttings in a small suitcase and took them down to Central London.

The auctioneers offered to put them into auction, but I decided to sell them directly. It was a highly emotional decision, and I was very anxious that I was doing the right thing, knowing these precious medals were going into a private collection, but the auctioneers assured me they would be well looked after. I walked out of the auctioneers, incredibly upset, as the medals had meant so much to Laurence and part of me felt I'd betrayed his trust in selling them. If it wasn't the right decision, I would never be able to forgive myself, get the medals back, nor ever see them again.

Laurence's medals, listed in the Appendix.
(Jan Scott)

The consequential dilemma I now had was how to spend the medal money? Laurence and the 21st IPC Club had developed a strong relationship with the Airborne Assault Museum, where I'd taken

Laurence for his 'Grand Day Out'. So, I contacted the curator Jon Baker at the museum, just at the time they were looking for funding to build an attention-grabbing museum entrance fit for the importance of the history of the Airborne Forces. It consisted of a mock up part of a Dakota aircraft door, with film of a paratrooper exiting, in various uniforms worn throughout the years.

And so, the medal money was donated to the Airborne Assault Museum. Eventually the grand opening day came in March 2016. Relatives of some of the pathfinders attended, along with veterans and museum staff. Jon Baker made a very moving speech, and after showed me a wonderful brass plaque at the museum's entrance. It read 'fuselage display was kindly funded by Ms Jan Scott in loving memory of her father Cpl Laurence 'Solly' Scott GM 21st Independent Parachute Company'. It was a kind and fitting tribute to Laurence and the pathfinders. I think he would have been surprised and humbled to see how he'd been honoured, and that the sale of his medals had made such a great contribution to the museum and airborne forces history.

As I embraced the relief I felt at helping to ensure Laurence achieved his 'great and happy trail', I realised the next mission was looming on the horizon: what to do with his Parachute Regiment Wings?

As I held my father's small, embroidered Parachute Wings in the palm of my hand, it was hard to take in what they had been through. Carefully sewn onto Laurence's uniform in 1942, they'd been on his arm as he fought for his life as a twenty-four-year-old, in occupied Oosterbeek. Their simple image of pale blue embroidered wings attached to a rather crudely embroidered parachute on a khaki background, belied the enormity of what they and their owner had gone through. As Lieutenant General Harrison had said, in his great speech given at the 2023 Arnhem Commemorations and quoted at the beginning of this book, Arnhem has become famous in history for the bravery of the men who fought there. It's become the 'go to' battle to inspire soldiers going into contemporary theatres of war. The wings had a job to do: inspire the following generations of soldiers and pathfinders and there was only one place they should go, back to where they'd come from: the Parachute Regiment.

Laurence's Arnhem Parachute Regiment Wings
(Jan Scott)

In July 2016, a pathfinders history day was organised at their Colchester home. Two of the original 21st IPC veteran's, Jim Chittenden and Peter Block, went to tell their stories of fighting in the South of France and Greece. Peter Gijbels, who had come over from the Netherlands and co-wrote the book *Leading the Way to Arnhem*, gave a fascinating talk on the original Pathfinder Company and their Arnhem experiences. At the event, I was very pleased to present Laurence's carefully framed Parachute Wings, to the pathfinders and they still take pride of place on their wall. Laurence was always very eager to talk to the younger soldiers whenever he could. They would circle round him, listening in silent awe as he told his experiences of soldiering and survival. He would be very honoured that his wings are now continuing to inspire the next generations of elite soldiers.

Fast forward to four years later, and a hot July in 2020. England, along with the world, was in the grip of the global Covid pandemic and the country had been in lockdown since March. In July, the lockdown restrictions were starting to be eased, but people had developed a different way of living, communicating and working online and through social media. This also applied to the bidding processes in the London auction house, where in February 2012, I had sold Laurence's medals.

On a July day, which revolved around the strange, yet stressful boredom of living in the Covid restrictions, my phone pinged with a message from Linda Bailey, an ex-police officer who knew Laurence from Hornsey Police Station and who had in his later years, interviewed him for the Metropolitan Police Oral History Project. Linda told me an officer from the Metropolitan Police had found Laurence's medals for sale on the auction site. He'd asked that the medals be kept in the Metropolitan Police, and there was a crowd funding campaign organised to try to buy them. Shocked, I looked at the auction house site where indeed the medals had come up for sale again. My heart did a leap with joy, but then anxiety set in: I could never afford to buy them back for the police. It was one of those moments where one has to trust in fate. So, I did.

Linda explained how another ex-police officer, Annie Gooch MBE, was running the online fundraising campaign, appropriately called 'Op Scott,' to try and buy the medals and so keep them in the police 'family'. Along with everyone involved with the campaign, I held my breath whilst messages passed to and fro, updating us on what was happening. On the auction day, the medals went way past their valuation, with a hammer price of £11,000. We heard Annie wasn't sure they could purchase them, then through her, and other officer's constant hard work, and hundreds of donations from current and ex-Metropolitan officers and police organisations, a 'lockdown' miracle happened. On 16 July, Annie messaged to everyone, 'OMG… we did it… those medals are coming home.' Everyone was in tears with relief. It's fair to say that I was completely astounded at the campaign, and incredibly grateful for the generosity of everyone involved. Yet I'd known deep down, that somehow Laurence's medals would find their way home, and to their rightful place. It's thanks to Annie, and Metropolitan Police officers, past and present, that they did. They are now in the collection of the Metropolitan Police Museum, at Sidcup, as an exceptional collection of medals, and as an example of the bravery shown by Detective Sergeant Laurence Scott and that required of all police officers.

There is no doubt that Laurence's 'great and happy trail' is still happening in many surprising ways, and will continue long into the future.

Laurence and his daughter Jan, at the 2004 Arnhem Commemoration
Sunday Service.
(Michael Compton, 21st IPC)

I'll leave the last words to Laurence, Solly, my dad. After Peggy had
passed away, he always sat with his George Medal where he could see
it, resting next to his mug of tea, on his small table in its scarlet, white
silk lined case. He was both proud and humbled that he'd received the
medal, it was a validation of a lifetime of truly remarkable bravery, but
there's no doubt that his wartime experiences were those which had
the most profound impact upon him. I remember when we were
chatting one evening and I asked what he felt was the thing, apart from
beloved Peggy, that meant the most to him. He spoke five words which
encapsulated how he'd risked his life to save his family, to try and
liberate the Dutch people, to defend and protect his pathfinder
comrades, and preserve democracy for future generations. With a flash
of determination and pride in his eyes, the fierce soldier still within him
even at the age of ninety, he said, 'I fought for my country.'

APPENDIX

List of Laurence's Medals:

George Medal EIIR
1939-45 Star
Italy Star
France and Germany Star
Defence Medal 1939-45
War Medal 1939-45
General Service Medal 1918-1962, with clasp, Palestine 1945-48
Police Long Service and Good Conduct Medal EIIR

BIBLIOGRAPHY AND REFERENCES

Army.mod.uk, *Paratroopers Remember the Original Red Devils*, 12 November 2022.

Brentjens, Jory, *Fled to Fight-The Jewish refugees of 1st Airborne Division*, WBooks, in collaboration with Airborne Museum, Oosterbeek, Zwolle, Netherlands, 2023.

Census records of 1921.

Gijbels, Peter and Truesdale, David, *Leading the way to Arnhem*, R.N. Sigmond Publishing, Renkum, Netherlands, 2008.

Glenton, George, *12 Years for Lone 'Wolf Boy'*, *Daily Mirror*, p.22, 19 November 1964.

Grandeguerre.icrc.org, *Prisoners of the First World War*, the ICRC archives.

Groeneweg, A, *Monument for the 21st Independent Parachute Company*, Friends of the Airborne Museum, Newsletter No., 4 November 1981.

Hansard, H. C., Deb 14 October 2019, Vol. 666, *Battle of Arnhem: 75th Anniversary.*

Kent, Ron, *First In! Parachute Pathfinder Company*, B. T. Batsford Ltd, London, 1979.

Kirby, Dick, *The Brave Blue Line-100 Years of Metropolitan Police Gallantry*, Pen and Sword Books Ltd, Barnsley, 2011.

Newark Advertiser, Red Berets are Reunited, 31 May 1975.

Nottingham Guardian, Escapers Held After Tip-off, 9 June 1966, p.7.

Paradata.org.uk, Lieutenant Herbert David Eastwood MC, Airborne Assault Museum.

Partington, Walter, *Gun -point Hero*, *Daily Express*, 15 February 1967.

Scott, Laurence, handwritten letter about his time in Italy, unpublished, 25 August 1995.

Scott, Laurence, *My Early Days in the Army*, printed in the 21st Independent Parachute Club Newsletter, issue number and date unknown.

Scott, Laurie, (Solomon), North Africa, typed notes.

Scott, Laurence and Peggy, various notes, letters, and recollections, private collection.

Scott, Solly, *A Norwegian Saga*, 21st Independent Parachute Company Club

Newsletter, No. 15, December 2004, p.15.

Stebbings, Peter, *Remembering a Bridge Too Far*, Times Group Newspapers, 16 September 2004, p.31.

Taylor, Caroline, *Time to Take the Wife Out! Says 'Lol'*, *The Journal*, 22 March 1985, p.11.

The Birmingham Post, *Grisly Finds in Sewer May Reveal 16 Killings*, Special 20th Century edition, January-June 1983, 28 December 1999, p.21.

The Gazette (London Gazette), Second Supplement, issue 44248, 10 February 1967.

Van Eck and Oosterink, *Airborne 60 jaar herdenken, Years of Commemoration*, Dodewaard, Netherlands, 2004.

White, Jerry, *Rothschild Buildings, Life in an East End Tenement Block 1887-1920*, Pimlico, London, 2003.

ABOUT THE AUTHOR

Jan Scott's creative work has been influenced by her family living through two world wars. She curated a World War 100 exhibition in Colchester, and produced a short film on the Battle of Arnhem, with the Airborne Assault Museum, IWM Duxford. In 2014, she was involved in the funding and production of BIFA award winning and BAFTA nominated film, KAJAKI.

Living in London, Jan is concentrating on writing, having studied creative writing at Faber Academy, and had her short stories published. Follow Jan at @Jan_Scott44.

Printed in Great Britain
by Amazon

46325888R00050